PRAISE FOR

INTERCESSORS

God is calling His people to pray, to seek Him, to listen for His voice and to press into Him with personal concerns, community matters and global issues. This book contains godly wisdom for guiding your prayers.

BILL BRIGHT

Founder and President, Campus Crusade for Christ
Orlando, Florida

An exciting book for strategic times! World evangelization requires powerful prayer warriors. This is a landmark work that can help godly men and women to reach their full potential as dynamic agents in the release of God's power. *Intercessors* is a must-read eye-opener for all in the Body of Christ.

LUIS BUSH

International Director, AD2000 & Beyond Movement
Colorado Springs, Colorado

Intercessors takes deeply serious prayer material and makes it accessible to the common, everyday person. This is a book you can give to both your newly saved aunt and your on-fire youth pastor!

FRANK DAMAZIO

Pastor, City Bible Church
Portland, Oregon

This book is a wonderful gift to all believers.

TED HAGGARD

Senior Pastor, New Life Church
Colorado Springs, Colorado

This book reveals how God has uniquely prepared every single one of His children to carry out a life-giving work of prayer. Use this book to find your own path in prayer. Use it to honor and encourage others in prayer.

STEVE HAWTHORNE
Director, WayMakers
Austin, Texas

Intercessors is a manual for those who may not believe they are intercessors simply because they cannot relate to the classic intercessor's mold. This book will draw out your unique anointing and will keep you from comparing your assignment with those of other intercessors.

CHUCK PIERCE
Vice-President, Global Harvest Ministries
Colorado Springs, Colorado

This book helps us to stand confidently in the gap for the people and issues He alone places on our hearts. I highly recommend it to all serious prayer warriors!

QUIN SHERRER
Author of *Good Night, Lord*
Colorado Springs, Colorado

The effective functioning of the Body will be greatly enhanced as each of us understands his or her personal prayer job description. I highly recommend this book—a unique learning experience.

THETUS TENNEY
Coordinator, World Network of Prayer
Tioga, Louisiana

Just about everyone I meet these days wants to be part of the incredible prayer movement we are seeing all around us. This book will open the door for you. Read *Intercessors* and you will find yourself lifted into new horizons of power in your life.

C. PETER WAGNER
Chancellor, Wagner Leadership Institute
Colorado Springs, Colorado

INTERCESSORS

*B*UT TO EACH ONE IS GIVEN
THE MANIFESTATION OF THE SPIRIT
FOR THE COMMON GOOD.

1 CORINTHIANS 12:7

ELIZABETH (BETH) ALVES · BARBARA (TOMMI) FEMRITE
& KAREN KAUFMAN

Regal

A Division of Gospel Light
Ventura, California, U.S.A.

Published by Regal Books
A Division of Gospel Light
Ventura, California, U.S.A.
Printed in the U.S.A.

Regal Books is a ministry of Gospel Light, an evangelical Christian publisher dedicated to serving the local church. We believe God's vision for Gospel Light is to provide church leaders with biblical, user-friendly materials that will help them evangelize, disciple and minister to children, youth and families.

It is our prayer that this Regal book will help you discover biblical truth for your own life and help you meet the needs of others. May God richly bless you.

For a free catalog of resources from Regal Books/Gospel Light, please call your Christian supplier or contact us at 1-800-4-GOSPEL or www.regalbooks.com.

Cover and Interior Design by Rob Williams

Permission has been granted for the use of all personal stories and letters. In some cases, names have been changed to protect the privacy of the individuals.

LIBRARY OF CONGRESS CATALOGING-IN-PUBLICATION DATA
Alves, Elizabeth, 1938-
    Intercessors/Elizabeth (Beth) Alves, Barbara (Tommi) Femrite, Karen Kaufman.
      p. cm.
    Includes bibliographical references.
    ISBN 0-8307-2644-6
    1. Intercessory prayer—Christianity. I. Femrite, Barbara, 1947- II. Kaufman, Karen, 1946- III. Title.

BV210.2.A47 2000
248.3'2—dc21   00-059249

1 2 3 4 5 6 7 8 9 10 11 12 13 14 15 / 09 08 07 06 05 04 03 02 01 00

Rights for publishing this book in other languages are contracted by Gospel Literature International (GLINT). GLINT also provides technical help for the adaptation, translation and publishing of Bible study resources and books in scores of languages worldwide. For further information, contact GLINT, P.O. Box 4060, Ontario, CA 91761-1003, U.S.A. You may also send e-mail to Glintint@aol.com, or visit their website at www.glint.org.

$\mathscr{C}$ONTENTS

Every Christian Contributes
*The people out front need others cheering from behind as much
as the ones who are behind need the leaders out front! Each person has an intercessory anointing that needs to be extended as a
lightning rod for change.*

Standing Against Injustices
*Your issue is what makes you weep and pound the table, but it
must always be motivated by love.*

The Balcony People of Prayer
*List pray-ers' passion for structure brings freedom for them-
selves, encouragement for others and the reward of perseverance
from above.*

God's Midwives
*God's midwives of prayer stand in the gap for people who must
choose between everlasting acceptance and everlasting rejection.
They fight for those who need a family and a home.*

Spiritual Guardians
*Personal intercessors are trusted by God to carry confidential
information in and out of the throne room for another in order to
partner in that person's protection, provision and prayer priorities.*

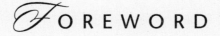

FOREWORD

You *must* read this book! "Another book on prayer?" you might ask. The answer is a resounding, "Yes, thank God!" as well as an emphatic, "No—not *just* another book on prayer!"

I am constantly amazed at the continuing amount and deepening levels of revelation God is bringing to the Body of Christ on this crucial subject. It is as though a well of revelation has been uncapped and, the more the Church draws from it, the purer and stronger the flow becomes.

While we have had much *defining* of prayer and intercession in recent years, it appears to me that we're moving into the *refining* and *assigning* phase. The army is moving from boot-camp to the battlefield and from the classroom to the war-room.

All biblical truth must move from an understanding to an application. So often this never happens, and the sad result is knowledge without wisdom, hearing without doing, noise without power and potential without fruit. There is an obvious determination of the Holy Spirit that this doesn't happen with the worldwide prayer movement. Thus, we have books like the one you're holding in your hand.

I'm not prophesying—but I am ready to make a bold prediction—this book will become a best-seller. And it will be instrumental in bringing the prayer movement to a new level. Many potential pray-ers, having been awakened to the power and need of prayer, will now begin to find *their* places on the wall. This is why of the many recent books on prayer, *Intercessors* will ultimately be seen as one of the most important and beneficial. Thank God for it! Even as I write this foreword, I find myself both thrilled and humbled to have a part, however small.

I am well acquainted with the three instruments chosen as the conduits of this gift to Christ and His Warrior-Bride. Beth Alves, a genuine mother in Christ to my wife, Ceci, and me, was moving in prayer before the movement of prayer. She, and others like her, birthed the rest of us. How fitting that she be a part of this treasure!

Then there is her disciple, Tommi Femrite, also a dear friend of Ceci's and mine, who quickly grew from student to teacher and from disciple to mentor. Watching her grow from soldier to officer in the prayer army has been almost dizzying in speed and power. What a powerful warrior and teacher!

And what can I say about Karen Kaufman, my God-assigned editor of *Intercessory Prayer*? She helped an upstart, fledgling, wannabe author break through the soil as a tender-shoot writer. Her understanding, encouragement and expertise became midwives for my ministry as a writer. To have the privilege of serving her in this small way is a fitting honor.

To the three of you, I can only say thanks for this priceless work. The army can now be better positioned, and the Captain can assign the troopers with greater precision. Frustrated warriors, who have tried to wear armor that didn't fit, will now pick up the stones, fit them into their slings and slay the Goliaths of their world.

The Son asked for the nations as His inheritance (see Ps. 2), the Father said yes, and books like this are part of the plan—saved for such a time as this! So are you, dear saints of the highest One. You are the soil into which these powerful seeds are about to be sown. Handle with care and then let the reaping begin!

DUTCH SHEETS
Colorado Springs, CO

ACKNOWLEDGMENTS

Thank You, God, for our husbands Floyd Alves, Ralph Femrite and Dennis Kaufman—holy men who have shielded us with their love and strengthened us with their encouragement.

Thank you

- for our precious families that have helped to sculpt our lives and taught us more about You;
- for faithful personal intercessors who have sacrificed on their knees so we could birth this message;
- for the dedicated staff members of Intercessors International who have shared the vision and served tirelessly to complete the mission;
- for the heroes of the faith whose stories have made this book a reality;
- for the dedicated staff members of Gospel Light Publications: Bill Greig III, Kyle Duncan and David Webb, who believed in the message; editor Deena Davis; Kim Bangs, Pat Bear, Billie Baptiste, Alice Coryell, Anita Green and Flora Washburn for being intercessory watchmen; Nola Grunden, whose efficiency keeps the process running smoothly; Rob Williams, who added his own unique skills to make the cover and interior design shine for the Kingdom;
- for Jeanne Senecal who did an excellent job of transcribing our tapes;

- for the many shepherds who have enriched our lives:
Burton Stokes, Olen Griffing, Dutch Sheets, Ted
Haggard, Jack Hayford, Larry DeWitt, Bob Olthoff,
Bayless Conley and Rick Warren.

Most of all, thank You, Father, for the marvel of being used
to accomplish much for Your kingdom through prayer.

Every Christian Contributes

∽

Introduction

Kittens are a rare sight in Africa, but that fact doesn't stop nine-year-old Abahu Odakonda from wanting one. Within her small frame is a big heart that longs to share affection. Jon, the English missionary who lives in her remote village, has come to share Jesus with Abahu's family. Her father grunts with disgust each time news of Jon's visit echoes a warning from native drumbeats of nearby witch doctors. Patiently and daily, Jon asks his heavenly Father for a plan that will soften the calloused hearts of these unsaved villagers.

Often he stops by the Odakondas's shabby little dwelling to extend some sort of kindness, but he has no idea that an eavesdropper named Abahu is drinking in the message. Jon's eyes glisten with a genuineness Abahu has never seen before. His words drip with love about a God she has never known. Jon's God is a giver, a provider—or is He? She has to know for sure. Silently, hopefully, she dares to mouth a short simple prayer for a kitten, in Jesus' name.

Jon has no idea about Abahu's desire for a kitten; he only knows that God alone can answer the cry of his heart to bring

Jesus to this secluded jungle compound. Then one day while Jon is deep in prayer, he hears the helpless meowing of his own furry little feline just outside his window. Not wanting to interrupt his conversation with the Lord, Jon tries to ignore it. But the desperate sounds of need continue to tug at his heart. He steps outside and notices the kitten tethered to a branch at the top of a tall, narrow sapling. As usual, Jon drops to his knees to pray. "Father in heaven," he exclaimed, "how can I get this kitten down?!"

He glances at his truck and remembers that he has left a rope sitting on the front seat. Scrambling to grab the rope, Jon finally calms down enough to string it from the bumper on his truck to the trunk of the tree. With the sapling on one end and the truck on the other, he plans to bow the tree just enough to stretch forth a rescuing arm to the frightened kitten tucked within its frail branches. Snap! With eye-popping disbelief, Jon watches the tree whip back into upright position, flinging the kitten through the air with the speed of a discharged bullet.

On the other side of the village, Abahu has gracefully perched her ebony face in the palms of her hands while gazing into the distant clouds above. You guessed it! Out of the heavens come the sad meows of a terrified kitten that plops into a nearby shrub. Abahu screams with joy as she snatches up her miracle and runs to tell her dad. Struggling to catch her breath, she gasps, "Daddy, Daddy! Jesus is real! He dropped a kitten out of the sky just for me!" Straining not to show emotion, a single lonely tear spills down Mr. Odakonda's cheek. The softening of his heart has just begun.

In the meantime, Jon is searching under every twig and leaf, cutting through the surrounding foliage and asking God's forgiveness for his obvious indiscretion in caring for his pet. He wonders if he has failed God. Has God heard his prayers? Darkness blankets the terrain and Jon is forced to give up the search. Stretching his tired body across the primitive mattress of his bed, this mercy-charged servant of God drenches his pillow in tears before falling off to sleep.

Word of Abahu's miracle travels fast, and the next day Jon is invited to her father's hut for a meal. With his daughter joyously beaming at his side, Mr. Odakonda acknowledges the goodness of God and whispers a childlike prayer of belief: "Jesus, come into my heart." Five simple words spoken in faith transform a household and eventually save an entire village.

The Bible says that when just one soul is saved, all of heaven rejoices (see Luke 15:10). Why so much celebrating for just one soul? As we read the story of missionary Jon and the difference he made in the Odakondas's village, it's easy to see how his loss became Abahu's gain. What we don't see is the entire host of people who contributed to Jon's success: teachers who prayed and taught him; leaders who sacrificially denied themselves to be role models for him; prophets who listened and encouraged him; and many different prayer anointings that linked in intercession to empower his missionary work and usher in his mighty anointing.

ANOINTING?

Confusion about the word "anointing" has caused much controversy in Christian circles today, and yet an anointing is simply the release of God's power through us to passionately sustain doing what we cannot do in our human strength. The flow of His power as He anoints us is much like standing under a showerhead. We choose to stand unclothed under the control of the showerhead to receive its cleansing power. Similarly, as the Head of the Church,

Jesus will pour His power in and through us when we choose to restfully enter His presence and shed the clothes of self-effort.

Your intercessory anointing is the area of your prayer life that is intended to be a lightning rod for change. Each one of us has a prayer-power mix that we cannot earn, but we can carry to the assignments God has set apart for us to do. As you read through the chapters that follow, our hope is that you will discover your prayer-power mix, the anointing that causes you to stand fully aligned with your mission field in prayer.

Know the Condition of Your Own Field

You do know that you have a mission field in prayer, don't you? If not, it could be that you have been comparing your field with someone else's. Sadly, we have seen many people who were called to be great intercessors, but they did not discover their anointing because they were too busy examining the fruit in another person's prayer field.

Will you take a moment to lay down this book and look at your thumb? There is no other thumb like it on the face of this earth. God gave you a print that is uniquely identifiable to you. You are one of a kind, "fearfully and wonderfully made" (Ps. 139:14)—not to be compared with anyone else. You were born an original; don't try to become a copy! When you pray, ask the Lord to show you how you are to be different from—not the same as—other intercessors.

A great salesman once said that when you are selling an inferior product, you compare similarities; when you are selling a superior product, you reveal its uniqueness. God's Word tells us that when we compare ourselves with others, we are "without understanding" (2 Cor. 10:12). Comparison leads to competition and envy (see Jas. 3:16) and destroys unity in the Body of Christ. Only when we fully appreciate the unique portion we have to contribute in prayer are we fully able to celebrate the glory that others carry.

One of us is not better than the other—just different. As Christians, we don't live to imitate each other; we live to imitate Christ. Likewise, when we pray, we don't do so to sound like others; we pray what the Holy Spirit says to pray.

No More Knitting Socks

Imitation happens in the prayer room because too few Christians take the time to intimately know the heavenly Father and find their own anointing in prayer. Anne Ortlund once told the story of a young college girl who was so busy with her studies that she didn't have time to call her father. With Christmas vacation approaching, Dad invited his young collegian to spend a week with him at the family's mountain retreat.

They both arrived the same day, excited about the visit. On the surface all seemed well when they greeted each other, but the daughter ran off to her room. For four days she remained behind closed doors. The father sat, quietly yearning for his child's attention, refusing to intrude upon her privacy. Finally, the day before Christmas, the young woman burst forth from the bedroom with her hands behind her back, giddily exclaiming, "Daddy, wait till you see what I've done for you!"

She quickly presented a pair of socks. "Daddy, for four days I have been in my room knitting these gorgeous socks for you. Look! Aren't they beautiful?"

The father lovingly embraced his daughter, with tears coursing down his cheeks. Then he replied, "Honey, I could have bought socks anywhere. What I really wanted was time alone with you!"[1]

Many of us today long to find our prayer place in God's kingdom on Earth, but we have been so busy knitting socks—doing good works—that we have not learned how to hear His heart. Prayer is the priority—not works. None of us wants to get to heaven and find that we have knitted socks for the Father but neglected His heart over our mission field in prayer. Let us therefore set aside our own agendas to hear the Father's voice and know who we are to support for Jesus' sake.

It's a Wonderful Prayer Life

Do you remember the film classic *It's a Wonderful Life*? In the movie, a distraught businessman named George Bailey meets with a clumsy-looking angel named Clarence, who is working arduously to earn his wings. George flings himself off a bridge, hoping to end his misery forever; then he hears the splashing and frantic yells of Clarence, his guardian angel. The problem: This angel can't swim! George, a man whose heart pumps with mercy, simply cannot refuse the summoning cries from Clarence's staged drowning. The unlikely twosome form a bond. George is then granted the rare opportunity to see how life would have looked if he had never been born. He later realizes his value and accepts the fact that he has a place of importance in the lives of others.

Like George, we need a new perspective. No power on Earth gives more importance to the Body of Christ than prayer. Each one of us has people whom God has placed or will place on our hearts to lift up in prayer, but we must make the choice to pray for them. When time as we know it now resounds with its final tick, the Book of Life will open and we will see the faces of all who have sacrificed to bring forth the purposes and plans of God in our lives. We will also see the difference our prayers made or could have made in the lives of others.

Think about that as you read the following letter.

A Martyr's Letter

Dear Ones:

Well, considering how hard Satan has fought our work, I am actually praising God that I am still alive. I live on all of Paul's writings (1 Cor. 1; 2 Cor. 4; 2 Cor. 6), realizing firsthand that a true servant suffers afflictions, tribulations, hardships, hunger, sleepless nights—all have become a part of my life.

I led three powerful seminars with Mozambique pastors and have never seen such hungry hearts. Mozambique (north) now has more martyrs than any other country in the world. I have literally walked in their blood but never have seen such worshiping, victorious Christians.

While attempting to reach the border to meet with 100 pastors, we lost one truck, two cars and two motorcycles to the enemy, but the Lord was with us. We are walking in victory and many are being saved.

I met a man who said, "I live in caves and hills. I wear the skins of animals, but the love of Jesus keeps driving me further into Mozambique. I am hunted like a wild animal by soldiers. They will kill me eventually, but I count it an honor to die for the One who died for me."

A man and many pastors were coming out to meet me, but the enemy intervened. Nine pastors were shot—eight killed and one wounded. After another seminar, 17 pastors were arrested. One of them said, "We have had no clothes or food for months, but I didn't come out for food or fellowship; I came to hear the Word of God. And when I go back I don't ask for food—only Bibles." We had no Bibles to give him. Many pastors don't even own a Bible here.

We live in a village where we sleep on the ground with no blankets in the cold of winter, and live like the Mozambiques.

The spirit of love has fallen everywhere. It reminds me of Pentecost.

I met one man who had his hand cut off for holding a Bible and his ear cut off for hearing the Word of God. He was then made to eat them. His lips were later cut out for preaching. But he stood up, shining, and said, "I now preach with this hand, hear with this ear, and my mouth will sing Jesus' praises." He began singing out, "Hallelujah! Hallelujah!" in unclear sounds.

One pastor had to provide shelter for 30 widows within a month's time. Their husbands were all killed for their faith.

What is our part here? To fill the hearts of those ready to die and watch over hundreds being saved under their ministries.

I have seen many Marxist soldiers saved as they watched God's glory fall on the Christians they were killing. I will never be the same.

We need your prayers more than we need your silver or your gold. You are a key in this hour. Please, won't you help us?

All Pray, But Not All Pray the Same

Each of us will have a different response to this letter, based on the anointing God has given us in prayer. The perfect prayer meeting for this martyr, however, will include the concerted, focused prayer anointings of the entire Church:

- List intercessors will begin to hold this dedicated missionary up daily.
- Personal intercessors combined with list pray-ers will know this missionary's schedule better than he knows his own.
- Leader intercessors will pray for the needs of the missionaries, pastors and rulers.
- Salvation intercessors will cry out for the souls that need to be saved.
- Financial intercessors will believe for the money to send carloads of Bibles.
- Crisis intercessors will tune in with an ear that is open to God's SOS alerts to trouble.
- Mercy intercessors will respond with tears of compassion and deep anguish in their souls.
- Warfare and research intercessors will fight the demonic forces at work by uncovering and breaking spiritual strongholds.
- Worship intercessors will release worship to usher in the glory of God in that place.

- Issue intercessors will summon heaven for religious reformation.
- Family intercessors will intercede for the widows and children left behind.
- Governmental intercessors will pray for the leaders of the country to effect change.
- Church intercessors will pray for the ministry and teaching there.
- People-group intercessors will drop to their knees for the Mozambiques.
- Prophetic intercessors will speak forth proclamations and do prophetic acts to penetrate the spiritual ground in the heavenlies.

All of these anointings will be needed to cause God's kingdom to come and His will to be done on Earth. One person's prayer power will leave off where another's anointing picks up. Prayer anointings are much like the tulip fields of Holland. From a distance, all the purples, for example, look the same; but a closer inspection reveals their distinctive shades. Likewise, each person's individual anointing will have prominence, but to reflect the full heart of God, it must blend with the beauty and power of the anointing of others. This perfect blend of prayer power causes the Body of Christ to become a field of answered dreams from the Father's heart in heaven.

Every Christian has a piece of God's heart to pray in prayer and His power to carry as we present the whole Body of Jesus to a lost and dying world. Whether called to stand on the front lines or to provide a support team at home, it takes every single one of us to win a village to God in prayer.

Lessons from a Goose

We can learn a lot about building a strong force for God by studying the animal kingdom. Geese, for example, travel in a rotating V formation. One goose flies out front to bear the brunt of the wind until it begins to lose strength. Then another goose moves to the forward position. The purpose of being in first place is not to look the best; it is to help all the others reach their destination. Studies show that the reason geese honk while flying is to encourage the one that is temporarily in front.

Like the geese who bear the winds of adversity on the front lines, spiritual leaders, pastors, missionaries, business leaders and government leaders need the rest of us to take our rightful positions in the V, or victory, formation—to encourage, warn and support those who are called to the front. By doing so, we discover that we too are prepared to move forward with strength when God calls us there.

The blood of martyrs throughout the world cries out: We don't need your silver and gold, we need your prayers! Will you help? Will you hold up your lightning rod of power and shock the world with the love and unity of Jesus?

Let's join forces and see what God can do as we honk encouragement to those in front of us and build each other up in prayer!

PERSONAL REFLECTION
Have You Discovered Your Anointing?

1. Can you think of times when your intercession has joined with that of others to bring about change?
2. Using our definition of "anointing," can you think of times when your prayers have been anointed?

3. Have you been "knitting socks"? If so, will you commit to finding your power rod of prayer and letting the Father show you where to use it?

4. Are you comparing yourself to another intercessor? Instead, will you decide right now to celebrate your differences?

5. Can you think of anyone God has called to the front lines who needs your support today? Will you pray for that person, even if that individual receives more "honking" than you?

Note
1. Anne Ortlund told this story at a retreat for Bethany Baptist Church of Thousand Oaks, at Arrowhead Springs, California, in 1997. It has been adapted for this book.

CHAPTER 1

ISSUES INTERCESSORS

STANDING AGAINST INJUSTICES

Twelve burly fishermen climbed into a large seaworthy whaling boat. Three were headed north, three south, three east and three west. When the large, rugged craft finally forged into the open seas, tension began to mount as each trio rowed toward their own destination. The hefty wooden hull began to spin about like a dog chasing its tail, while every man fought frantically to hold his own position. Before long, the oars became weapons of destruction rather than tools for navigation. What might have been "fellowship" turned into mutiny among the "fellows in the ship." Finally, the whole uncharted mission sank as the vessel capsized and broke apart in a swell of confusion and defeat.

Sounds ridiculous, doesn't it?! Many times, however, the fellowship at prayer meetings looks a lot like what we've just described—especially when praying over issues. One person wants to pray about the abortion issue, another about pornography; someone else wants to prayerfully tackle gambling issues, while another seeks a solution for families. Before long, a power struggle ensues and no one feels heard or honored. The intercessors limp out of the prayer room feeling bruised and battered, never wanting to set foot on that ship again.

No More Mutiny in the County

Now let's replay the saga of our 12 brawny fisherman with a new twist. Imagine what could have happened had these trios of ambitious sailors set course in four separate boats with only one focus as their destination. Not only would they have reached their targets, but they also would have bonded in a spirit of unity along the way.

When teaching on corporate intercession, we begin by asking the pastor to identify issues of concern, such as missions, feeding the poor, schools and youth—the list could be endless. Next, we gather the intercessors and ask the Lord to speak to each of their hearts regarding the concerns at hand. Various parts of the room are designated as meeting places for each issue. Everyone is then asked to identify and write down the concerns that kindle a passion in their hearts. Issues and passions are finally linked together as a three-strand cord forms for what author Evelyn Christensen calls "triplet praying." Whether 4 or 400 respond to a given issue, that number eventually splits into clusters of three. One of the triplets leads in verbal prayer while the other two agree; each person then takes a turn at the prayer helm. Triplet praying ensures safety for those who might otherwise be intimidated by public prayer. It also helps intercessors to more fully understand the heart of God over a particular issue.

Identifying Your Issue

Those who pray over issues will find that the Holy Spirit imprints an assignment on their souls. Sometimes issues flow out of their own hurts; other times the Lord simply drops a burden, like a seed, into the heart's soil and then pours out prayers to water it.

Carol Ann Ferrell is one of those people who began her assignment through fresh pain. Several years after coming to Christ, a woman from church handed her a picture of a six-week-old fetus. Having had two abortions that resulted in permanent damage to her womb, Carol Ann finally understood that not only had her actions destroyed her own hopes of ever having a family, but she had also killed two little babies. For three days she sobbed without ceasing. When the tears finally stopped, Carol Ann knew that God had cleansed her of all shame and was calling her to intercede for other young women with a potential for following in her footsteps.

She poured herself out daily in her prayer closet, and once each week she put feet to those prayers by standing in front of a local abortion clinic to pray on-site. Throughout the four-year duration of that assignment, Carol Ann saw more than 20 women reverse their decisions. One young girl even asked her for a ride home and, on the way, confessed that she was pregnant with twins. Though Carol's mission was rewarding, when the Lord removed the burden, the grace and power to intercede for that issue also lifted.

Her next assignment began when she inherited an apartment building in Los Angeles, California. Rapes, murders and drug transactions were a daily occurrence in the alley just behind her newly acquired building. Raised in a wealthy family, Carol Ann had never understood the hopelessness and despair that drove the downtrodden into lives of uninterrupted crime; but as she interceded for them, judgment was overshadowed by mercy. The inner city became her mission field in prayer. She "prayer-drove" the streets and prayed God's Word over the hurting. Though her life was often in peril, Carol Ann saw the hand of God move on her behalf. Eventually, she was even able to summon local law enforcement to change laws which brought greater protection to that area. The assignment lasted 10 years.

Today Carol Ann intercedes for the leaders in her church. Because she is also a list pray-er, she has pages and pages of Scriptures she prays daily over each leader. Sometimes the Lord will reveal a problem or expose a spirit that is trying to get a foothold, and she will pray until the burden lifts. In her own words, "I don't know how long this assignment will last or what the next one will be—that's up to God. I will simply pray what He gives me to pray until He moves me on to the next issue."

Issues That Define a Lifetime

An issue of intercession can also become a lifetime assignment. Eva Alexander, for example, was a powerful politician in India when she received Christ as her Savior. Today, as director of The Comforter Ministries, she says that her lifetime issue began when she read, "Assuredly, I say to you that tax collectors and harlots enter the kingdom of God before you" (Matt. 21:31, NKJV). She then heard the inaudible voice of the Lord assuring her, "You shall see the harlots in heaven." Those words echoed within her head, because prior to her conversion, Eva had supported prostitution by lobbying for legislative policies and programs that would protect it.

Now, realizing that she was to be part of seeing the harlots in heaven, Eva began to travail on their behalf. "God," she cried out, "I have a heart for these women. But, Lord, I don't want to reach just a few of them, I want to reach every single one—every temple prostitute, every call girl, every street prostitute. And when I get to heaven, I want to see millions of them there. I want to hear the words, 'Well done, thou good and faithful servant.' I believe You have forgiven me for the sins I committed in supporting prostitution before I knew You. Now use me in any way You desire to protect the harlots and bring them into the Kingdom."

Eva invested much time in prayer before sharing the vision with her husband. When she finally did, he agreed to stand with her in that effort. Their mission began with hours and hours of intercession, but they had no idea how great the cost would be. They brought the prostitutes home and began to pray over them, counsel them, teach them, provide medical care for them and help them find jobs. Some returned to the streets many times before the love connection with Jesus became a reality, but Pastor Eva and her staff refused to give up on even one. She pursued them by walking the streets and openly sharing the good news about God's love and forgiveness.

Eva's family and staff suffered persecution from neighbors as well as government authorities. They were ridiculed and mocked, even harassed by those who accused them of running a brothel. But Eva persevered, saying, "If God gives the mission, He will also provide for its success."

A prostitute she had ministered to later confessed that while conducting an immoral act, the radio alarm next to her bed went off and a pastor said, "Woman, your sins are forgiven!" Immediately, the woman left that lifestyle. Today she is an effective evangelist in India.

When Pastor Eva began the ministry, "sex workers," as she calls them, had no means or desire to care for their babies. She took the issue to God in prayer. Initially the children were sent to Mother Teresa's orphanages that in turn sent prostitutes to Eva's ministry for counseling. This exchange continued until the Lord intervened through intercession with a new plan. Today The Comforter Ministries (TCM) operates the Rachel Home for Babies and El Shaddai Children's Home. Many have been victims of prostitution and kidnapping; others are born to sex workers who have not yet met Jesus. TCM lovingly raises these boys and girls to be prayer warriors, teaching them how to fast and pray for the ministry.

Intercession is still the core of Eva Alexander's life. Following God's orders, TCM now offers an AIDS Awareness program, providing counseling for families, eunuchs, transsexual workers, homosexuals and lesbians. TCM is, at the time of this writing, prayerfully waiting upon the Lord for the funds to build a shelter for AIDS and HIV victims who have nowhere else to go.

Pastor Eva will often dress up as a temple prostitute to enter the temples where 10-year-old girls are being dedicated as temple prostitutes and raped by the priests. Her mission is to pray for them and pierce the darkness with the love of Jesus. Though these young girls are discarded by temple priests at age 18, they are regularly rescued by TCM.

When Pastor Eva and her staff first began to invade the lonely streets where sex workers pandered their counterfeit love, pimps attacked them verbally and sometimes even physically, doing immeasurable damage to their property. Today their work receives the approval and support of local law enforcement, and some of those same pimps have joined their ranks as ministers of the gospel.

Standing Against Injustices

Issues intercessors are those who stand against injustices. Their prayer-power mix often combines with mercy and/or warfare to fight for those who can't fight for themselves. Only when love is the driving force behind issue intercession is there enough passion to finish the assignment.

*O*nly when love is the driving force behind issue intercession is there enough passion to finish the assignment.

One of the board members for Intercessors International, who has invested her life in praying and working for the oppressed, is Beverly McIntyre. The first 16 years of Beverly's biography are steeped in every imaginable kind of abuse. But the neglect, rejection and violence of her childhood has also been an incredible gift, providing keys of identification that open doors to tightly locked hearts. Beverly is a champion of the downtrodden, who says that the call upon our lives is what makes us weep and pound the table. We'll let Beverly talk:

I can't bear to see people oppressed or slighted or judged for their outward appearance. I agonize over the complacency and discrimination within the American Church because we pick and choose those we do and do not want to minister to. We'll give our money but not ourselves.

My intercession is almost always for the unsaved, the downtrodden, the weak, the poor. I weep and pound the table when people for whom Jesus died go unnoticed. It appalls me to think that few people in the Body of Christ are praying for or caring about those people. For me that includes abortion doctors and nurses, homosexuals, prostitutes and everyone else that most of the Church would like to ignore.

Beverly is a dedicated issues intercessor whose assignments start at the feet of Jesus in prayer and end in accomplishing missions that most people would be afraid to tackle. She has prayed for and ministered to alcoholics and drug addicts on the streets of Baltimore and entered the war zone of Croatia five times to minister to Bosnian refugees. She works with battered and homeless women and children in Arizona and embraces hurting women at conferences throughout the world. In this chapter, however, we want to highlight a family issue that is near and dear to Beverly's heart—her daughter's battle with bulimia and anorexia.

Once again, Beverly tells the story:

My daughter was unmercifully chided and teased about her weight as a child and grew up with a lot of shame regarding her body. Later, in her teen years, Satan finally wrenched a deadly grip on her life. Though the pendulum swung back and forth between bulimia and

anorexia, it began at age 16 when Crystan started binge-
ing and purging. I had no idea then that we were the typ-
ical family in which eating disorders are usually bred: my
husband *was* an emotionally distant father; I *was* a con-
trolling mother. For years, I walked a co-dependent
pathway with Crystan, checking the toilet after she ate
and monitoring her every move. I sought help from
every Christian counselor and friend who offered the
slightest hope in holding the key to her healing.

Finally, when Crystan turned 22, I faced one of the
darkest days of my life. My husband and I checked our
daughter into a secular clinic that secured her behind
locked doors. Leaving that hospital, I felt devastated
over her pain and my inability to intervene with a solution. For several days I did nothing but sob. I knew at
that point that our only hope was Jesus. As I cried out to
God, the Lord impressed me to pray Isaiah 54.
Throughout three of the four weeks of her hospital stay,
I walked the floors for a minimum of eight hours daily,
proclaiming Isaiah 54 over her life and declaring that
bulimia and anorexia would have to bow to the name of
Jesus. One day, a peace eclipsed my pain, and I knew the
work had been done in the heavenlies.

The time Crystan spent in the clinic had steeled her
feelings of anger toward me and everything I represented. My daughter returned home embittered and hardened to the things of God. For three months I simply
rested in the peace God had given me. Suddenly, at
about 2 A.M., I was awakened by the sounds of weeping
as my daughter discreetly tiptoed into my bedroom.
"Mom," she sighed, "come and hear what the Lord just
spoke to me." I followed her to the kitchen and listened

attentively as she read Isaiah 54 from the *Amplified Bible*. I did not tell her then nor did she have any idea that not only was this the same Scripture I had prayed over her, but it was also the same version I had used. Crystan crawled into my lap, and God healed her that very night. It was a defining moment for both of us.

Today when people tell me they have addicted children at home, I encourage them not to become sedated by victimization but to rise up with mercy and fight. Draw a line in the sand and tell Satan he can't cross over it, because God has given you the authority to fight in His name. Become a prayer weapon for God until that child experientially walks in the victory of Isaiah 54:13: "All your children shall be taught by the LORD, and great shall be the peace of your children" (*NKJV*). No one will ever love your child as much as you do. You are the one who is called to pay the price in prayer. Find a Scripture and stand upon its truth until the Lord gives you the assurance that the breakthrough has happened. Don't give up. Don't look at what you see. Instead, stand upon the Word and focus upon the Lord's power. Trust God to save your family.

Family Issues—the Foundation of Our Nation

All issues eventually affect the family, and whatever affects the family will ultimately affect the nation and vice versa. Issues intercessors are, therefore, those who most often prayerfully ban together to fight for change in laws that govern the nation. Dee Jepsen, for example, is a woman of prayer who served in 1982 and

1983 as the special assistant to President Ronald Reagan, acting as a liaison to women's organizations. God used Dee to kindle the smoldering embers of concern regarding pornography in America, an issue that is offensive to both active feminists and conservative Christians alike.

By 1990, Dee had recruited a small but determined army of women to intercede against the pornography issue. As word of her concern spread, Dee was contacted by a lady from Ohio who rallied together a cross-cultural group of women for a conference in Washington, DC. Dee spoke at that meeting and eventually became president of Enough Is Enough. The organization's mission was initially to combat illegal pornography. It now fights to protect children from pornography on the Internet that could render them prey to pedophiles.

Enough Is Enough had a major role in effecting the passage of Senator Exon's Communications Decency Act (CDA). Though the bill was initially slated for failure, Enough Is Enough hosted a luncheon on Capitol Hill, stormed the offices of local politicians and even alerted media attention to the savage debauchery being promoted over the Internet toward children. Although the ACLU and other liberal groups successfully fought to overturn the bill in the Supreme Court, the CDA helped to stimulate people's awareness of child pornography.

Dee Jepsen confesses that she spent so much time interceding and battling against the diabolical spirits blanketing child pornography issues that her joy and ability to hear God's voice were extinguished for several years. There is a price to pay for fighting over these issues, but no matter how high that price, our children are worth it. They are tomorrow's politicians and prayer warriors, but they need our intercession today! Just one look at the graphic smut Satan is promoting over the Internet is enough to permanently stain a child's mind. The battle is great and the workers are few, but prayer is the key.

Satellite groups of prayer currently stationed throughout the United States continue to hammer away at this firmly entrenched cancer in the Internet world. In the often quoted words of former United States president Ronald Reagan, "The world has yet to see all the great things that can be done when nobody cares who gets the credit." Issues intercessors are among that group and we applaud their efforts to secure and perpetuate the safety of our children.

The Key: Unity

Whether the issue is children, widows, singles, blended families, abortion, pornography, education, political concerns or something else, the key to praying for issues is to align with those who have the same focus, who walk in agreement and are like-minded.

The key to praying issues is to align with those who have the same focus, who walk in agreement and are like-minded.

Jesus said, "If two of you agree on earth about anything that they may ask, it shall be done for them by My Father who is in heaven" (Matt. 18:19). In Genesis 11, we read the story of men who united to build a tower for an unholy purpose. God said that because "they are one people. . . now nothing which they purpose to do will be impossible for them" (v. 6). If that is true of the unrighteous, how much more will we who are seeking God's plans and purposes be able to accomplish when we pray as "one people" with one voice and one issue as our focus?!

Pitfalls of Issues Intercessors

Focusing on the positive side of our prayer power is only one way to discover our anointing. Have you noticed that our positive attributes also have a negative side? That is true of intercessors as well. The very strengths that are given to catapult us into victory can also plunge us into problems. We call these negatives pitfalls because when we fall into one—it's the pits! But sometimes we can discover our strengths by studying our potential for weakness.

Aligning with the wrong people is only one of the potholes, or pitfalls, that attempt to puncture our prayer tires as we pick up momentum on the highway of intercession. Others include:

- Becoming frustrated or angry with others who do not share the burden over the same issues
- Thinking that our issue is the only important issue
- Wearing the issue as a red badge of courage that can even turn to pride
- Allowing the issue to become so consuming that the Lord takes second place
- Wanting to rescue based on a soulish love rather than a call of God
- Exceeding the boundaries God has set for helping
- Becoming so filled with the negativity surrounding the issue that the spirit becomes dry and parched

- Letting people's lack of appreciation supersede God's call to arms
- Succumbing to guilt and confusion when the issues outweigh the number of laborers
- Isolating from, rather than aligning with, others who have the same issue
- Praying for the praise of people rather than the praise of God—the One who assigned the issue in the first place

KING LEMUEL'S MOM, OUR PROFILE IN ISSUES INTERCESSION

Helen Keller said that physical blindness is not nearly as bad as having sight without a vision. She saw with the eyes of the heart and changed issues that affected those around her. As both biological and spiritual parents, we have an incredible responsibility to provide vision for those we mentor so that they will fulfill their purpose upon the earth.

Clearly, King Lemuel's mom was a woman of vision who fought against the injustices of her time and trained others to do so as well (see Prov. 31). She was a woman who fulfilled her promises to God and even called her son a name that meant "belonging to God" or "devoted to God." This virtuous woman took a godly stance regarding many issues and even provided a prototype for the ideal Christian woman, which all aspire to today. The issues she faced are those that beckon our attention even now:

- sexual impurity (see v. 3)
- alcohol/drugs (see v. 4)
- legislative injustice (see v. 5)
- defending the oppressed and needy (see vv. 8,9)

- protection of marriage and the family (see vv. 10-22)

Within the first nine verses of Proverbs 31, we can clearly identify King Lemuel's mom as a Dee Jepsen, advising the president about the moral issues of her day, or a Beverly McIntyre, fighting against the injustices of the poor. She may have been a woman in politics, standing against abortion and working for sexual abstinence in the schools. The hope for her son may have been for him to become a Josh McDowell, who has devoted his life to preserving the sexual purity of America's youth, or a Dr. James Dobson, who has fought both legislatively and on American radio to preserve the family.

We don't know exactly what role she would have fulfilled today, but her instruction is clear: "Open your mouth" (vv. 8,9). The following are some of the ways we believe issues intercessors are called to open their mouths. Read through Proverbs 31 and see if you can find others:

- Open your mouth in prayer for those who do not have a spiritual voice yet.
- Open your mouth for those who are unfortunate and don't understand their spiritual authority or Kingdom rights.
- Open your mouth for those who are being afflicted by the adversary.
- Open your mouth for those who are spiritually needy.
- Open your mouth so that God can fill it with His wisdom and revelation knowledge.
- Open your mouth before the King of kings so that you will know what to say in the presence of worldly leaders.
- Open your mouth with words of trust and praise so that you will have the faith to face trials and temptations.

- Open your mouth with words of virtue and worship so that you will leave a legacy.

Choose to spend time at Jesus' feet, speaking for those who cannot speak for themselves. In the process of laying your life down for the issues that concern others, you may find that your mouth is filled with a voice that rings down through the ages as that of King Lemuel's mom. The Lord said, "Open your mouth wide and I will fill it" (Ps. 81:10).

Shout against injustices and God will shout His praises over you!

PERSONAL REFLECTION

Are You an Issues Intercessor?

1. Do injustices against others cause you to mount up in prayer?
2. Can you think of something worth prayerfully fighting for that flows out of your own or someone else's hurtful experience?
3. Where do you see people crying out in hopelessness and despair?
4. Has God provided you keys of identification to open doors into tightly locked hearts? If so, do you realize that you are also called to pray for those people?
5. Are you a defender of any or all of the little children of the world?
6. Can you think of something that makes you pound the table and weep? Are you opening your mouth for that issue?

CHAPTER 2

LIST INTERCESSORS

THE BALCONY
PEOPLE
OF PRAYER

Many years ago a famous singer was contracted to perform at a Paris opera house for one night only. Within days the event was sold out and the entire city was abuzz with anticipation. When the long-awaited evening finally arrived, a reluctant house manager took the stage to announce, "Ladies and gentlemen, thank you for your enthusiastic support. Sadly, the woman you've come to see has taken ill. We do, however, have an incredible substitute who will provide you with comparable entertainment."

The crowd groaned so loudly with disappointment that few even heard the singer's name. Frustration replaced excitement in the hall. And though the stand-in singer gave everything she had, her final bow was met with cruel silence rather than gracious applause. Suddenly, a child stood up in the balcony and shouted, "Mom, I think you are wonderful!"

The crowd immediately responded with a thunderous ovation.[1]

We all need people in the balcony to cheer us on and pray for our success. List intercessors are the balcony people of prayer. They are dependable and they strengthen us with their loyalty and unwavering love. They are the children of God who shout, "I think you're wonderful! Keep on going! You can do it! I've got you covered in prayer!"

If one particular group of intercessors were to receive an award for perseverance, it would be the list intercessors. Many times a list pray-er will know your schedule better than you know your own. If you are on the list and you have been told you will be prayed for every day at a particular time, rest assured, you will be.

WHEN ONE PERSON'S LIST BECOMES ANOTHER'S LOSS

Problems arise when one person tries to force another to imitate his or her anointing. Intercessors International, for example, was invited to teach on prayer at a Bible school in North India. The president of the school operates solely as a list pray-er. Therefore, based on his own anointing, he insisted that every student arise at 4:00 A.M. daily to pray for one hour over the list he had compiled the day before.

When Tommi arrived, the students were discouraged and bored with prayer. Many confessed that if they received a request that touched their hearts, they found no difficulty interceding with great zeal. To their dismay, that one issue could fill most of the hour; but fear of being rebuked kept them from lingering over the particular prayer request they felt moved to pray for.

This school president, like most list pray-ers, believed that only regimented prayer could be effective. Pastors and Sunday School teachers usually teach this kind of prayer, thinking it is the only way to pray. Consequently, many Christians have erroneously decided that because they don't pray from lists, they are not intercessors. List pray-ers tend to be more effective when praying independently; thus, they can frustrate the mix of anointings in a group. Those who are created with a need for diversity find list praying—especially over another person's list—inhibiting, confining and boring.

*M*any Christians have erroneously decided that because they don't pray lists, they are not intercessors.

As a matter of fact, when Dennis and I (Karen) first began to set time aside for joint prayer, I thought his "prayer needle" was stuck in a rut. I could not believe that my husband was praying the same Scriptures over the same list of people every single day . . . after day after day. God will often add new people to his list, but some have remained on it for years and will stay on it until the Lord tells him otherwise. If you are on Dennis Kaufman's list, you will be prayed for tenaciously and with consistent predictability.

A list pray-er is someone who will pray about any subject you provide, but he or she prefers to have a list to follow.

You're Never Too Old

Ruth A. Garlock was a dear list pray-er who has now gone on to be with the Lord. She and her husband married on the mission field of Africa in the 1920s and left a rich legacy. The Lord gave them a list of missionaries for whom they faithfully prayed daily. Anyone in ministry who knew about their list coveted a place on it.

Several years before Mrs. Garlock died, she mused, "Honey, I have outlived everyone on my list but one. Oh, well! I guess that's a good thing because I couldn't see to read my list anymore, but I'm not too old to remember one name!"

Not All Lists Are Prayed the Same Way

Though we tend to think of list pray-ers as those who jot their prayers on paper, not everyone does. Dennis, for example, dictates into a pocket tape recorder the verses and burdens on his heart for his listees. His recorder is a reminder to pray throughout the day; it also provides a vehicle for recording special insights from the Lord.

The breadth of ingenuity in list intercession has yet to be exhausted. Quin Sherrer, coauthor with Ruthanne Garlock of *How to Pray for Your Children*, calls herself a Scripture pray-er. For nearly 26 years, Quin has preserved her prayers in yearly journals, which she divides into five sections. The first section hosts a picture of herself with her husband, LeRoy, along with their personal prayer Scriptures. The next three sections are dedicated to the families of their three children—detailed with photos, Scriptures and prayer requests for each person. Quin assures us that recording the date beside answered assignments is a holy faith booster!

The final phase of her journal is reserved for her sphere of influence. Quin laughingly calls this section her "bean patch," based on 2 Samuel 23:11,12:

And the Philistines were gathered into a troop, where there was a plot of ground full of lentils [beans], and the people fled from the Philistines. But he took his stand in the midst of the plot, defended it and struck the Philistines; and the LORD brought about a great victory.

Quin insists that we all have a bean patch to stand watch over for the sake of the Kingdom. Her plot of spiritual ground includes unsaved relatives, young missionaries, pastors, spiritual leaders and political issues. Though Quin's list is a coveted place for anyone who needs prayer, she has learned through "Prayer Burnout 101" that only the people God assigns are to be on that list. A bulletin board hangs over her desk with pictures, notes and verses, reminding her throughout the day to take a prayer stand for those in her victorious lentil fields.

The List Map

Another person who has added a new spin to list praying is a young mother named Alicia Eckman. This energetic new mom constructed a list map of her immediate neighborhood, then asked the Lord for a Scripture to plant as a prayer seed of faith over each house and began the process of harvesting spiritual ground. With a list map taped to the hood of her baby's carriage, Alicia would set out at the same time each day to prayerfully cover nearby homes with God's life-changing Word.

One house in particular tugged for her attention. She noticed the yard in desperate need of grooming and discovered the Lord had given her healing Scriptures to pray there. For weeks Alicia spent a little extra time stopping to intercede in front of that home. Finally, prompted by an urge to uncover Alicia's motives, the resident of the house approached her. When Alicia explained that she was simply praying, the lady's face brightened with hope. She told of her husband's illness and invited Alicia inside to pray over her husband; the man recovered remarkably soon afterward. Today this neighbor joins Alicia on her walks, knowing firsthand that God's Word does not return void (see Isa. 55:11).

Lists Can Lift You into Your Ministry

Any discussion about list pray-ers is incomplete for me (Beth) if it does not include the mention of my spiritual mom and mentor, Vinita Copeland. This beloved woman of God was the biological mother of a prodigal who was seeking and attaining his fortune as a worldly musician. When his records began to lead the charts, his publicist distributed 3 x 5-inch glossies of the industry's prominent new star. As mothers do, Vinita maintained a stack of those pictures in abundant supply. But instead of using them for "brag boards," this celebrity mom was distributing them as a prayer request at every Christian conference and prayer meeting she attended. If you received her son's picture, you were expected to pray. Her persistence paid off; today he is one of the leading evangelists in America.

The pain Vinita experienced over her own son led to a picture prayer ministry for prodigals. Women throughout the states would send her photos of their unsaved children and ask for prayer. Daily she lifted those faces before the Lord, believing God that the hearts of these children would return to the heavenly Father. I can hardly wait to hear heaven's head count of those she prayed into the Kingdom!

Freedom in Structure

One of Intercessors International's dependable list pray-ers, who has often accompanied us on prayer journeys, is Mary Napier. The following interview with Mary gives keen insight into the life of a list pray-er.

I find freedom in structure. When I have structure—things lined up, in order and written down—I am free to think about the rest of my life, knowing that I won't forget important obligations. For instance, I will often invest a few minutes at the beginning of a week or holiday season to write down everything I need to accomplish within that time frame. I then plug those activities into my calendar.

With regard to my prayer obligations, I save them in myriad forms. I collect monthly newsletters, e-mails and Post-It Notes. I keep these "lists" in my place of prayer. Many are detailed with a finish date, which I adhere to; later, I simply toss that paper away! Others I will pray over until I feel "a release" in my spirit—no more unction to pray. Some, however, will remain on my prayer list until the Lord Jesus comes for me or I go to Him.

When people learn that I am an intercessor, they often ask me to pray what I refer to as "on the run." This term simply means that they will stop me, share their story, ask me to pray for them and then run. I learned from a very wise lady, Quin Sherrer, that I don't need to feel obligated to "on the run" lists. I simply say that I will pray at that moment, or I ask them to put it in writing. None of us really has the time or passion to pray for everyone and everything. So if it's important that "I" pray for that person's need, I believe he or she should be willing to take the time to write it out.

If I feel impressed or have the time, I will seek the Lord for a "word" or a Scripture for those on my list. Then, when God responds to my seeking, we are both blessed. The Lord doesn't spoil me with His revelation every time I ask; however, I am always faithful to deliver the word promptly when He does.

Occasionally, I feel overwhelmed by the numerous scraps of paper—lists—that beckon for my intercession. And yet, I know that my God answers prayer in His time. Eventually, each one of those needs will be prayed through and replaced by new ones. Isn't God good?!

So that no one will pale, thinking that the list pray-er spends EVERY morning locked in a prayer closet, allow me to add a word of caution. I, too, have those days when I am required to be out of the house very early. In my observation, few people have the privilege of spending every early dawn to pray and seek the Lord. So when I am unable to invest time in detailed intercession, I cover those for whom I have accepted responsibility with the life-giving blood of Jesus and ask Him to hide them from the enemy. If I feel "burdened" and still don't have the time to sequester myself, I symbolically place them before the Lord and pray in the Spirit until released to move out into God's project for me that day.

GRACE FOR THE LISTS OF THE LISTLESS

Though many of us are not list pray-ers, at times God will require us to submit to our leaders by praying over lists. As we surrender our wills to that authority, we can be sure God will cover us with the grace to obey. I (Tommi) attend New Life Church where my pastor, Ted Haggard, rips the pages out of our local telephone directory and lays them on the steps of the platform. Each person in the congregation then picks up one section so that every person in our city is prayed for by name for one week. The last time I participated in this form of list praying, I found the names of two people I knew on my page. It was exciting to realize God had customized my list.

Similarly, Floyd Alves (also a crisis intercessor) will comb the sports pages to discover athletes in need of his intercession. For example, when Floyd read that Michael Jordan's missing father had regrettably been found dead, he began to pray for Michael's physical, emotional and spiritual health. The prayers escalated when Floyd heard that Michael was abandoning basketball for good. Convinced that this was the wrong decision, Floyd continued to prayerfully intervene on Jordan's behalf until two years later when his basketball career was finally reestablished.

Not only do list intercessors gather their sources differently,

Your heart attitude is always more important to God than your performance in prayer.

they also sort that information in unique ways. Some list intercessors divide their lists into topics such as salvation, healing, finances, individuals, family and leaders. They will then assign one day to each topic. Others hold their lists before the Lord, seeking His direction for the person or issue that is on His heart.

List pray-ers can spend hours praying Scriptures over those the Lord has assigned to them. Everyone on the front lines should have the prayer backing of at least one list intercessor.

PITFALLS OF LIST PRAY-ERS

The discipline we see in list intercessors can cause us to think their prayer lives are flawless. Not so. Some of the pitfalls list pray-ers must beware of include the following:

- Believing there is no other way to pray while modeling this type of prayer in corporate settings
- Becoming judgmental toward those who deviate from the list
- Declaring that God doesn't speak to them in prayer
- Lacking compassion over a list compiled by another person
- Allowing their lists to be so important that they miss what is on the Father's heart at the moment—especially in corporate prayer meetings
- Being determined to pray through the entire list each time they pray
- Experiencing condemnation when they don't pray the entire list
- Letting the list become so long that futility causes them to give up prayer altogether
- Becoming overwhelmed and frustrated when their lists continue to grow without seeing answers to prior requests
- Lacking the boundaries to say no to those whom God has not ordained to be on the list

After reading about these pitfalls, you may be thinking, *That would never happen to me!* But have you ever noticed that when Satan comes to buffet your prayer life, he does it with a fatiguing tenacity? His strategy is to oppose you so much with condemnation and discouragement that you quit praying completely.

Whether you are a new list pray-er or a veteran, be sure to extend grace to yourself. Your heart attitude is always more important to God than your performance in prayer. And though you have been created with a need for structure, that structure must be flexible enough to be remolded by your Maker. Every mission has a season, and every season has its missionaries, including list pray-ers.

Ezra, a Man After God's Own List

The Bible gives us a profile for the list pray-er in the biography of Ezra the scribe. Believed to be the author of most of 1 and 2 Chronicles as well as Ezra and Nehemiah, this noble man of God records lists in all of his writings. In the book of Ezra, he lists those who returned to Jerusalem, the heads of the clans and those who were involved in mixed marriages. Clearly, these people were the concern of his daily prayer life. God used him to purge His people of idolatry and spur a great revival. We have gleaned the following lessons from Ezra's example and hope you will read his story to discover even more:

- Honor your covenant with God and others on your list.
- Set priorities for your times of prayer.
- Be disciplined.

- Become an avid student of the Word, memorizing and praying it over those on your list.
- Record what you receive in prayer, including dates and details.
- Allow your love for Jesus to shape your prayer for His people.
- Under the Holy Spirit's direction, show others what you have received.
- Do not be afraid to confront issues of sin or call for repentance if the Holy Spirit directs.
- Allow the King of kings to reveal the mission and stick to it.
- Incorporate worship into your prayer time.
- Make your own purity a matter of priority.
- Be open and flexible to God's call to add or delete the people, places and issues that are on your list.
- Understand that not everyone is committed to lists, especially to yours.

For Ezra, freedom was spelled "list"! Faithful is the way God judged him!

—————— **PERSONAL REFLECTION** ——————
Are You a List Intercessor?

1. Do you find freedom in structure?
2. Would regimented prayer inhibit you or release you?
3. Have you recorded the dates of your prayer requests?
4. Do you pray over the same people consistently?
5. When called to pray for someone, do you start by making a list?

6. Can you identify with Ezra's love for lists and details?

Note
1. W. B. Freeman Concepts, *God's Little Devotional Book for Women* (Tulsa, OK: Honor Books, 1996), p. 49.

CHAPTER 3

SOUL INTERCESSORS

GOD'S MIDWIVES

Jesus said, "Go therefore and make disciples of all the nations, baptizing them in the name of the Father and the Son and the Holy Spirit, teaching them to observe all that I commanded you" (Matt. 28:19,20). This directive is what the Church calls the Great Commission, and all believers have a specific mission field to *go* to—both on our knees and physically—as we *co* or partner with God in the *mission* of discipling, baptizing and teaching. But before the mission of maturing disciples can begin, lost souls must find life in Jesus Christ by being spiritually birthed into His family. The Lord, therefore, has raised up men and women as midwives to pray "lost souls" through the birthing process.

I (Karen) will never forget the night my grandson Jason was born. My son-in-law was away on a military assignment and I had agreed to pray the baby through the birth process. Before each pain began, the needle on the fetal monitor would begin to slur, alerting me to pray. Though the birth contractions would register, prayer prevented my daughter from experiencing the full impact of the pain—without medication. It was much like watching an earthquake register eight points on the Richter scale with little evidence of any exterior shaking. For 13 long hours I stood beside Kjierstin's bed, praying and believing that God would bring forth new life. When the doctor finally rushed us into the delivery room, I felt as though I was a part of that child—I had labored in prayer and ached for his arrival. I had stood in the gap between the life my grandson knew in the world of my daughter's womb and the world he was now entering. I was a midwife, a "gap stander," for Jason Webber's physical life.

Spiritual Midwives

God's spiritual midwives move in deep anguish for souls to be born. They prayerfully stand in the gap between two kingdoms as lighthouses for those who are lost in the kingdom of darkness, directing them into the kingdom of light. Most people who are lost are seeking the right direction but don't know how to find it. Jesus said, "I am the way, and the truth, and the life" (John 14:6). Soul intercessors prayerfully travail until those for whom they are believing experience a spiritual birth into Jesus' way, truth and life.

Today, many pastors have established churches that are much like spiritual birthing rooms. We call these churches "seeker sensitive" because the atmosphere there is geared toward those who are still lost but seeking direction. When pastors with a message for seekers team up with intercessors who are burdened for souls, the results are exponential.

Intercession That Leads to Divine Intervention

If we are faithful to intercede for souls, God will usually call us out of the prayer closet to put hands and feet to the very prayers we have prayed. Our faithfulness in sitting at Jesus' feet will determine the strength and direction of our walk. Suzette Hattingh is one of the heroines of soul intercession who has graduated from the College of the Feet to walking for the Lord among the unsaved. Listen to her story as she tells it in her own words:

It was a bitterly cold and rainy Christmas Eve in Frankfurt, Germany. A few Christians and I had decided to be a blessing to some beggars that night, so we prayed and gathered several Christmas gifts for them. For some strange reason, we could not find the beggars—I do not know what God did with them that night, but they were nowhere to be found.

Deciding to search for them, we divided the group into pairs. Then, in a park across the road, I heard some voices. Crossing over to see if the beggars were huddling there to protect themselves from the rain, I walked into a divine appointment of God—not knowing that it would forever change the direction of my life!

As I approached the bushes where I had heard the voices, two men suddenly walked up behind me and pressed something sharp into my ribs. Instantly, I knew it was a gun. Taking a deep breath, I sighed an SOS prayer and decided not to show them that I was scared. At the time, I was a woman who fasted and sought God for revival and prayed passionately for the lost. But I always left the actual evangelism to someone else because I believed it "was not my gift." I assured myself that I was only called to intercession.

The men then asked me what I wanted. So with a straight face, I answered, "Nothing that you have, but you might like what I have!"

"And what is that?" they asked.

"A Christmas gift—that's all."

Surprised, they looked at me and removed the gun that was pushed against my ribs. They escorted me through the bushes and walked me straight into a drug den. A few hundred people were gathered there. At one corner, a prostitute was in full action, while a few feet away, some were buying and selling drugs. To my left, people were warming up heroin for their injections. Shock went through me like waves! I had never seen anything like it!

My coworker found a little boy who was screaming like a pig and pulling out his hair in bundles—totally wild! It took three men to hold him down.

When my coworker and I attempted to find out what was wrong, a man pulled us back and said, "Leave him alone if you want to stay alive!" They had just given him his first heroin injection because they wanted to make a child prostitute out of him—he was only about 10 years old! That rocked me to the core of my soul!

How blind we are; how little we care!

Suddenly, the voice of God spoke to me: "Where is the Church?" Where was the Church that night? Sitting around their nice little Christmas trees singing "Silent night, holy night . . ."! I realized that maybe the Church was too silent that night.

As I watched the desperation around me playing out like a scene in a drama from hell itself, the next question was: "Suzette, when did you last lead a soul to Me—not as Suzette the intercessor or as Suzette who works with the mission organization, but purely as Suzette the child of God—simply as a witness?"

That question hit me like a hammer! What was I to say to the Lord? If He had asked me when I last prayed through the night, I could have told Him. Or if He had asked when I had last prayed for the lost, I could have answered Him. But when had I last led a soul to Jesus? I thought that job was for the evangelist, and I was only an intercessor. To my shame I could not tell Him!

The scene of the little boy haunted me, the warming up of the injections, the prostitute, the hopelessness. . . . I made a decision that changed my life, promising the Lord that I would speak to everyone He sent my way. I started wherever I could—in the car, in airplanes, in shopping malls. It became one, then two, and has continued to grow since that time. I have now spoken to hundreds of thousands of people worldwide.

The appointment of God in that den of hell on Christmas Eve turned me from a woman of prayer to a woman of prayer and action! My life is given to prayer and evangelism—praying to the Father and seeking the lost.

Suzette's faithfulness in prayer for lost souls led to a ministry that resonates throughout the world. But that ministry was not birthed until God had worked His passion and purposes into her life. God's Word tells us that if we are faithful to humble ourselves under His mighty hand, He will exalt us at "the proper time" (1 Pet. 5:6). Timing is of utmost importance to God.

A Time to Be Born

Ecclesiastes 3 provides an in-depth teaching on God's timing, which is a major component in winning souls. Those who intercede for the lost know that trying to force a birth results in spiritual abortion, while waiting too long to call forth a soul can result in a stillborn death. God's midwives, therefore, will know the timing of birth through intercession and begin the process of laboring for souls. Then, because the foundation has been laid in prayer and intercession, those in the field need only call in the babes in Christ.

Jobst and Charlotte Bittner are seasoned soul intercessors in Germany who lead a ministry that does great works for God. Nearly five years ago, the Holy Spirit led them into a season of fasting and prayer in order to change the direction of their lives. Graciously receiving God's instruction to prayer journey the Chernobyl area of Russia, they packed their bags and awaited further direction. Another day of fasting revealed they were to focus on a secluded city they knew nothing about—Svetlagorsk. They obeyed.

Along the way, Jobst and Charlotte learned that Svetlagorsk had been closed during the Communist reign; people could not enter or leave its borders without permission. When they arrived there, these two faith-driven sojourners found that it was still neatly fortressed and could only be accessed by boat or bridge. They persevered. The Bittners tenaciously prayerwalked the city until the Lord guided them to a noisy restaurant that, by all outward appearances, qualified as an upholstered sewer.

Obediently, the two entered the restaurant and sat down to continue praying when the Holy Spirit burst upon the scene with a heavy sense of His glory. Both Jobst and Charlotte were overcome with God's love and mercy for the people and knew that He was calling them to make a difference in that raunchy den of sin. The presence of God continued to hover over them with such flaming power that they just sat there basking in His love till nearly 11:00 P.M. They left promising the Lord that they would not forget Svetlagorsk.

The following year, Jobst and Charlotte returned to host a Christian crusade there. Amazingly, local officials approached the Bittners to share some disheartening statistics about the city. They reported that Svetlagorsk had the third highest drug and HIV problem per capita in all of Russia; they also explained that because of the fallout from Chernobyl, most of the children were either dead or so badly damaged that the schools had been shut down. Jobst and Charlotte sought the heart of God in prayer.

In 1996, they sent a dedicated team of five to Svetlagorsk, led by a couple God had raised up in Minsk. The team spread the life-producing message of God's love and began to see many souls come to Christ. Today they have built a school and healing center where people are both physically and spiritually getting their needs met. Revival has sparked a steady stream of people— mostly drug addicts and HIV victims—who are daily being wooed to this place by the Spirit of God; once there, they receive a cup of living water in Jesus' name.

Amazingly, the school site was once a battlefield where Germans had killed many Russians, leaving deep strains of hatred. Today the sacrificial love of these Christian Germans is uprooting that malignancy so that God's redemptive love can minister deliverance and truth.

Svetlagorsk has become a beacon of hope to neighboring towns and villages as well. The villagers have all come to Christ; they now attend the school and serve at the center. Small groups are also being birthed throughout the land to minister to drug addicts and HIV victims. A once-forgotten city steeped in isolation and hatred has become a refuge of God's love because two obedient soul intercessors cared enough to pray.

Like the apostle Paul, Jobst and Charlotte have said, "I planted, Apollos watered, but God was causing the growth. So then neither the one who plants nor the one who waters is anything, but God who causes the growth" (1 Cor. 3:6,7). When soul intercessors pray, those on the front lines prosper and God's kingdom reaps the increase (see v. 8).

The Motivation

Someone once said that if you think the wages of sin are bad, wait till you hear about the retirement benefits! When a soul intercessor has fully grasped the atrocity of hell, that person has no choice but to cry out on behalf of those who will spend eternity there. Soul intercessors can be used to pray the worst enemies of

When a soul intercessor has fully grasped the atrocity of hell, that person has no choice but to cry out on behalf of those who will spend an eternity there.

society into the Kingdom, because they fully grasp the torment and flames that await the unsaved (see Rev. 20:10,14,15; 21:8).

The expression "Go to hell!" is as blasphemous as anything we can say because it defies what Jesus died to prevent. Will you stop now and ask God to give you a vision of hell? If you are a soul intercessor, this picture will motivate you to pray for the lost at any cost.

A burglar once confessed that before he attempted to crack a safe, he filed down the skin on his fingertips until they were sensitized to the click of the numbers on the lock. Likewise, motivated soul intercessors will often spend so much time poring over God's Word that they are spiritually sensitized to the appropriate Scriptures to pray over unbelievers. Because God has promised that His Word will not return void (see Isa. 55:11), the right verse is then used to crack the enemy's grip and set captives free.

The Spirit of Adoption

Lost souls are people who do not have a connection with the heavenly Father or His family. Though many lost people are financially very wealthy, without Christ they will be eternally homeless and never know the joy of entering into God's family as heirs. The need for material wealth is often their cover-up for a true sense of worth. Those who do not know Christ bear an eternal spirit of rejection. But Psalm 27:10 says that "when my father and my mother forsake me, then Jehovah will take me up" (*Amer. Std.*). No matter how rich or how rejected we have been, the Father's arms are open to all who will say yes to His spirit of adoption.

And speaking of adoption, Floyd was 26 and I (Beth) was a child bride of 17 when we married. (Floyd jokingly says he married me young so he could raise me right!) Even before we were married, we both began to pray for four girls. We were certain God had given us this desire. Then, in my late 20s, having given birth to only three children, doctors insisted I needed a hysterectomy! I felt empty for another daughter. I just could not shake the sense that one of the arrows God had intended to place in our quiver was missing (see Ps. 127:4,5). The void never left me.

In the meantime, a 10-year-old little girl named Sue was living with an alcoholic mother in squalid conditions in the Midwest. An Assemblies of God missionary to Native Americans, who lived next door to Sue, led her to Jesus and taught her how to pray. The missionary instilled within her the hope that if she would believe long enough and faithfully enough, God would one day answer her prayer to be part of a real family. Her prayer seemed to go unanswered.

One year later, the headlines of Oklahoma newspapers heralded a story of gross neglect. A starving 11-year-old girl had been found in a coma, weighing a mere 47 pounds. The victim was Sue. When doctors reported that this child would surely be blind or mentally disabled if she lived, the missionary who had encouraged Sue to keep believing gathered a group of Christians to set up a 24-hour prayer watch. Sue was in a coma for three months, but she woke up completely normal. The people who sat at her bedside praying throughout many long days and nights had reaped the benefit of their efforts!

Prayer spared her life, but tragedy would continue to weave strands of sorrow throughout the years that followed. As Sue moved from one painful experience to another, facing abuses that even now she hesitates to talk about, she decided the only way to become rooted in a family was to birth her own. At 17, she married and began having children.

Ten years later, I met Sue at a crusade in Africa, as part of an evangelistic team, but we had very little contact because Sue was intimidated by my prophetic gift—she was sure I would know everything about her. Three days later, however, while standing on the platform, I heard an inaudible voice clearly say, "Woman, behold your daughter!" Not knowing who was behind me, I turned around and locked eyes with Sue. As we gazed into each other's faces, Sue tearfully said she had just heard the words, "Daughter, behold your mother!" Much like the leaping that Elizabeth experienced within her womb when she met Mary, the mother of Jesus, something inside of me leaped (see Luke 1:41). Before long, we as a family had embraced Sue and her family as part of our own.

Then one day, as I was praying about an upcoming trip to Honduras, I was interrupted with a strong urging that we were to legally adopt Sue. Floyd and I prayed together and asked the Lord to confirm it. The first confirmation came while in a conference in McAllen, Texas. Without any solicitation on my part, the lady sitting in front of me began to tell of her adoption when she was 42 years old and how that experience had changed her life. Our second confirmation occurred when we called our attorney to inquire about adult adoption. He said he had previously arranged five adult cases. Then he asked why we wanted to adopt Sue. We explained that the Lord had brought this idea to us in prayer. Our lawyer confirmed our decision by telling us that five of his previous adult adoption cases were also completed because of obedience to prayer.

The main question was, Would Sue say yes to the adoption? When we presented the idea to her, she told us that she could not love us any more as an adopted relative than she did now. She went on to say that she did not want to burden us.

"Pray about it with your husband," I suggested. Her husband later called to say that he believed Sue needed some roots and that he was sure this proposal was from the Lord.

The court date was set. When we finally stood before the judge, he asked, "Are you sure about this adoption?" With one unified voice we responded, "YES!" The judge went on to explain the law regarding inheritance, which states that an adopted child can never be disinherited. He then said, "Sue will forever be legally entitled to one-fourth of everything you leave in your estate. She can never be disinherited. The laws that protect adopted children are far greater than the laws that protect biological children."

We signed on the dotted line and never looked back. On that day, a 10-year-old's prayers were answered as a young woman in her 30s said yes to her own adoption. Even though Sue's biological mother was eventually healed and their relationship restored, Sue belongs to our family. God not only answered the prayer of a child, but our prayer as well.

I tell you Sue's story so that you will understand what it means to be adopted into God's kingdom. You are an heir of all that He has. When God says, "I WILL NEVER DESERT YOU, NOR WILL I EVER FORSAKE YOU" (Heb. 13:5), He means NEVER!

Like Sue, God's adopted children are bombarded with new ways of functioning within their adoptive families. Struggles over family ways are sure to occur. But we who are mature must make the family a safe place where they can flourish. Let us not be guilty of neglect, especially in prayer. Let us instead move them gradually and gently out of the birthing rooms and into the acceptance of God's home where they, too, are called to be heirs.

Soul intercessors need to be the ones up front when the altar call is given. They should ensure that those who come to the Lord are given the good milk of the Word and, when needed, warm loving arms to comfort them. Part of the birthing experience involves making sure that new babes are passed on to loving shepherds. If you are a soul intercessor—one of God's midwives—before you leave the delivery room, pray for God to raise up others to nurse the newborns along.

Pitfalls of Soul Intercessors

Birthing is an arduous and fatiguing process—not only for the one being birthed, but also for the one who is standing alongside as a midwife. Let's take a moment to explore the pitfalls soul intercessors face:

- Feelings of futility over the number of lost yet to be saved
- Being discouraged from not hearing praise reports
- Judging rather than identifying with those who are in sin
- Experiencing apathy caused by an inability to understand the horrors of hell
- Falling prey to condemnation for taking on the personal responsibility of another's right to choose
- Being bored from repeatedly speaking the same verse to no avail
- Becoming fatigued from praying for days, months and years without results
- Lacking follow-through in prayer when a soul has been birthed

As we can see from this list of pitfalls, God's midwives are called to an extraordinary measure of persistence. But the fruit of that effort will last throughout eternity.

PAUL, GOD'S GREAT SOUL INTERCESSOR

No other New Testament character has been responsible for a greater soul count in heaven than the apostle Paul. His testimony is a timeless portrait of persistent prayer and prioritized passion. The record of Paul's night in jail with Silas (see Acts 16:16-34) is ripe with fruitful wisdom for today's soul intercessors.

Paul and Silas have just sustained a severe beating for silencing a demonized fortune-teller. Their torn skin drips with blood as they pursue the path that leads to the inner recesses of the prison. Locked in wooden stocks and chained like animals, Paul and Silas share their dungeon with what the courts have deemed to be the dregs of the criminal world. The stench is nauseating— the floors are covered with human debris.

Then, out of the bowels of inhumane captivity, prayer and praise arise as a tribute to God's unfathomable grace. Paul and Silas have but one focus: souls. Every ear is listening as the gentle calm of Paul's singing washes the atmosphere with peace. Suddenly, the stone foundations begin to quake, the doors fling open and the chains are miraculously loosed. A stunned and distraught guard is jolted out of a deep sleep. The guard, assuming the prisoners have escaped and believing he will be tortured for his failure to maintain his watch, lifts his sword to kill himself. But Paul stops him. Let's pick up here from the *New Living Translation*:

Trembling with fear, the jailer called for lights and ran to the dungeon and fell down before Paul and Silas. He brought them out and asked, "Sirs, what must I do to be saved?" They replied, "Believe on the Lord Jesus and you will be saved, along with your entire household." Then they shared the word of the Lord with him and all who lived in his household. That same hour the jailer washed their wounds, and he and everyone in his household were immediately baptized. Then he brought them into his house and set a meal before them. He and his entire household rejoiced because they all believed in God (Acts 16:29-34).

This story illumines the spiritual birthing process:

- Stay in fellowship and aligned with another brother or sister in Christ to maintain the focus of your mission; birthing requires support.
- Be prepared to confront evil at all costs, knowing that the price for souls can be excruciatingly painful.
- Pray for other laborers to come alongside the one you are praying for.
- Purify your heart, refusing to hold on to the hurts the unsaved inflict upon you.
- Focus on your mission rather than on the circumstances, realizing that delivery rooms are not usually comfortable.
- Create an atmosphere of peace through healthy denial by praying in God's presence.
- Remember that God's power is greater than sin's power and that "when a man's ways are pleasing to the LORD, He makes even his enemies to be at peace with him" (Prov. 16:7).

- Worship the Lord, knowing that music releases joy and "the joy of the LORD is your strength" (Neh. 8:10).
- Trust God's ability to create change.
- Expect some shaking of the old foundations before the captives are set free.
- Stay calm in the shaking, focused on the building and planting that will follow.
- Identify with the needs of the lost and extend hope and mercy when the shaking begins.
- Wait for a repentant attitude before you begin to minister change.
- Align with God for His timing.
- Know and proclaim the Word of God when the decision to accept Christ has been confirmed.
- Keep praying. Be sure the new babe in Christ has anchored his or her faith in fellowship with others before you stop praying.
- Realize that one birth will often result in multiple births, so pray for those within that person's sphere of influence.

Our responsibility is not to change others; it is to pray that circumstances will be aligned so that they have the opportunity to choose. When we enter into praying for souls, we enter into Christ's suffering. He died for all. But not everyone will receive His gift of salvation, and that truth is painful.

Our responsibility is to continue to go and tell until all have heard!

—————— **PERSONAL REFLECTION** ——————
Are You a Soul Intercessor?

1. Do you have a burden to pray for lost souls on a regular basis?
2. When you are with a stranger, do you find yourself wanting to know if that person is saved? Are you burdened to pray until he/she is?
3. Would you like to serve as an altar worker in your church?
4. Are the lost automatically drawn to you?
5. Are Scriptures for the lost easy for you to remember?
6. Does a seeker-sensitive church align with your call?

CHAPTER 4

PERSONAL INTERCESSORS

❦

SPIRITUAL GUARDIANS

Mama Cannelli was 89 years old when Dennis and I (Karen) first heard about her. The frailty of her body and the stench of her surroundings made us wonder why God would allow such a trusted saint to tarry so long upon the earth. Our reason for visiting her was part of a church outreach. We had no previous idea that tucked within the dark and depressing walls of the isolating rest home she called her missionary base was a light so bright that the Lord Himself refused to extinguish it. Though she was crippled by arthritis and spindly in frame, the passion of Mama Cannelli's call burned with infectious fervor.

Mama (as she was commonly addressed) had fragrantly lived most of her life in the background, summoning heaven with love's sweet aroma on behalf of others. Her mission as a personal intercessor was launched 60 years earlier, shortly after the birth of her only son. After laying her cherished little infant down for a nap, she picked up the local paper and read the stunning headlines: Sammy Havlerson Arrested for Armed Robbery. *Not Sammy!* Everything within her began to cry out, *No!*

Sammy was a PK—a preacher's kid. But he wasn't just any minister's child; Sammy was the son of Mama Cannelli's pastor. Her heart raced. She wept with a groaning so deep that only God could have plumbed its depths. For four days Mama fasted and pleaded with heaven on Sammy's behalf. Hope finally took root in her heart. Soon she realized she had been called to stand in the gap as a strong woman of faith for her pastor's boy.

Throughout the years that followed, she mailed him short motivating stories that she had written as a legacy for her own child and continued to encourage Sammy to complete his degree in prison. Year after year passed while Mama wrapped up the love of God in tenderly tufted letters that Sammy called notes from the lap of heaven.

Sammy was only the first of those whom Mama prayed out of prison and back into productive lives. When she would complete the prayer assignment for the one or two men God had laid upon her heart for the number of seasons He ordained, she then moved on to another. Her heavenly scrapbook bulged with spiritual sons who once had no hope—no place to anchor their dreams. She was a surrogate mother to those who felt orphaned, a friend to the isolated, a prayerful mediator for society's forgotten. Mama was a personal intercessor for those whose lives had been gnarled and marred by sin's livid onslaught. She is but one of the multitude who have sacrificed on beckoning knees to carry the faces of others into the throne room of God.

Leaders Need Prayer Too

Not only do personal intercessors have a burden for the destitute, but many have also been commissioned to prayerfully support leaders. At Intercessors International, we call them leader intercessors. The list of leaders we offer prayer support to include pastors, missionaries, spiritual leaders, various media people, sports celebrities, businessmen, governmental leaders and those in education.

Before we pair a leader with an intercessor, that intercessor is carefully trained and screened. Our leaders are assigned code names to preserve and protect their confidentiality. Only the leader and the people who oversee the prayer program at Intercessors International ever know the real name behind the code. No earthly contact is established between the intercessor and the leader. The intercessor receives a short biographical snapshot, disclosing only basic facts about the leader's family (i.e., how many children) and nondescript glimpses of the leader's ministry, business or position.

Every intercessor with this ministry makes a one-year commitment to pray for their assigned leaders for at least 15 minutes daily. Intercessors are provided with journal sheets used to record revelations from the Lord for each person being covered in prayer. Journal pages are then transcribed and sent monthly to the leader. A dedicated hotline provides the vital link for sharing confidential requests. And when we receive a warning from an intercessor for a leader, the staff prays over the validity of the message. If it is positively confirmed in prayer by two or three witnesses, one of our prayer overseers then contacts that leader.

Much of the intercession that sweeps through Intercessors International headquarters parallels the old television series "Mission Impossible." Some of our leaders live in perilous regions of the world that are restricted from any mention of Jesus Christ—to be identified as a believer could result in death. Therefore, our communications are so sensitive that they must be encrypted and destroyed immediately after being sent or received. The answers to prayer that we hear at our headquarters are nothing short of miraculous, and that is why we exist!

Praying On-Site with Insight for Leaders

At Intercessors International, not only do we intercede for leaders who contact us for prayer, but we also travel throughout the world to pray for those who don't even know they need it. Please permit me (Tommi) to explain.

After the war ended in Rwanda, I joined an international prayer team of nine prayer leaders from six countries (Malaysia, Singapore, Sri Lanka, Ethiopia, Kenya and the United States), led by John Robb of World Vision. Our mission was to establish an ongoing prayer strategy for Rwanda's leaders and to teach on the themes of forgiveness, reconciliation, God's love and strategic intercession (spiritual warfare).

What many people might not realize is that more than 90 percent of Rwandans are considered Christian. This nation was and is the pride of Africa. During colonial days it was divided into two ethnic groups: Tutsi and Hutu. The Tutsi were much taller and darker and considered more intelligent than the Hutu. Therefore, the Tutsi were educated and given great favors by the government, including positions of power—even in the Church. Later, ethnic status could be changed by acquiring wealth (defined by owning more than 10 cows), which allowed a Hutu to become a Tutsi.

Thirty years prior to the 1994 genocide that wiped out nearly 1 million Hutu within three months, war erupted and thousands of Tutsis were killed by Hutus. Family members in mixed marriages turned on other family members; neighbor rose up against neighbor and professed Christians killed Christians. The spirit of hatred had opened the door to all kinds of demonic activity in the land.

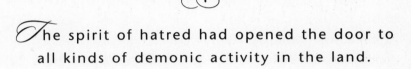

The spirit of hatred had opened the door to all kinds of demonic activity in the land.

On the third day of our trip, we prayerwalked the government buildings in Kigali, Rwanda's capital. When we arrived there, the team was divided into two parts. The group I connected with was in the process of praying throughout the main building when our host asked if we wanted to meet the president of parliament. We all eagerly agreed.

I was amazed to learn that this humble, gracious man in his early 30s was a Christian. We had barely set foot in his office when he began to ask, "Would you pray for me? I need wisdom. I need knowledge. I need to know how to successfully lead my country into restoration after the war between the Tutsis and the Hutus." Remarkably, I had just taught on identificational repentance and was sure this is what God had in mind for us to pray.

I explained to the others that as citizens of a country that was part of the United Nations, we Americans needed to repent for our country's refusal to intervene immediately in this conflict. We could have stopped the massacre, but we didn't! As a group we grieved over the sins of our nation and asked for forgiveness from the president of parliament.

Later, he wrote to us, asking us to relay any other spiritual discernment heard from the Lord on his behalf. A team member responded with a note, telling him that after leaving his chambers we had toured the city and learned that war erupted shortly after Rwanda accepted a statue from Egypt. The statue, which faces the government center, represents the goddess Ba and is a Phoenix bird with the countenance of a woman. We suggested the statue be removed. Much later, the president of the parliament advised us that he was taking steps to heed the warning.

Praying for governmental and spiritual leaders on-site with insight is one more reason that Intercessors International exists!

CALLED TO PRAY FOR BUSINESS LEADERS

Another important arm of the ministry of Intercessors International includes attending consequential meetings with high-ranking businesspeople to provide spiritual consultation. In one instance, I (Beth) was asked to fly to a restricted country to prayerfully offer spiritual discernment for a business consultant who is a part of my personal intercession. I recruited another intercessor to join me, and we were soon on our way.

The business consultant had been enlisted by the leaders of this nation to establish a training plan that would bridge business and government. As the consultant interviewed cabinet members and entrepreneurs, my friend and I would intercede to give both the positive and negative input the Holy Spirit revealed about each applicant. The Lord faithfully supplied wisdom to choose the appropriate candidates, and the program has brought incredible fruitfulness to that land.

We have found that businessmen who enlist at least one personal intercessor are much more likely to make right decisions and to experience the full blessing of God upon their company.

The Wise Personal Intercessor

Although we have concentrated on leaders in this chapter, personal intercessors are not necessarily focused on any one category of people. They are simply individuals who have been entrusted by God to carry confidential information in and out of God's throne room for another in order to partner in that person's protection, provision and prayer priorities. When God assigns one person to another as a personal intercessor, a heart response such as that of David and Jonathan begins to pulsate (see 1 Sam. 18:1). But just as important as the spiritual connection between these two people is the connectedness between the intercessor and God. Colossians 1:9 reveals the basis for personal intercession:

> For this reason . . . we have not ceased to pray for you and to ask that you may be filled with the *knowledge* of His will in all *spiritual wisdom* and *understanding* (italics added).

The Bible has much to say about the three-strand cord of spiritual wisdom, knowledge and understanding. Thus, if any one of these three strands is overlooked in personal intercession, problems can occur. We might have the *knowledge* of God's will, knowing what He wants a person to do, but lack the spiritual wisdom and understanding of heaven to back it up. In this scenario, human reasoning can take over and open the door to the enemy.

Wisdom is knowing God's timing and His plan for what He wants to accomplish. Without spiritual wisdom, we can do or say the right thing at the wrong time and bring about destruction instead of God's will. On the other hand, *understanding* is recognizing God's reasons for doing or saying something. When we have God's understanding, we have a pure motive and passion for completing His assignment. Motivation is that which moves us to action. Only when He fuels our actions do we have the strength and grace to joyfully finish the task.

Let's look at how these three strands—knowledge, wisdom and understanding—might affect personal intercession. You are praying for Bob when the Lord gives you a word of knowledge that he will be called to the mission field. Do you immediately dash to the phone and let him know what you've heard? Or do

Exposing God's secrets to manipulate others will usually cause the Lord to withdraw His presence.

you wait upon the Lord for spiritual wisdom to understand God's timing and plan for going to the mission field? Knowing the person you are interceding for is of utmost importance when deciding whether to release knowledge. Occasionally, God will use us to confirm what He has already spoken to another, but sometimes we are merely called to shoulder the knowledge in prayer. The Lord may simply ask us to carry a word like a seed until He is ready to birth it into that person's life. Our prayers then become the water for that seed so God can receive the glory.

As we wait for God's understanding to show us both our motive for sharing a word from Him and His motive for calling us into intercession, we may discover that we have had a personal agenda in wanting to share. Some intercessors want to share to get close to the one they are praying for; others share to exercise control in that person's life. But exposing God's secrets to manipulate others will usually cause the Lord to withdraw His presence. Even when God does allow an intercessor to share, the timing of that word is critical. Only the right word (knowledge) at the right time (wisdom) for the right reason (understanding) will bring about God's glory.

A Shield Against Deception

One reason the Lord provides personal intercessors is to prevent His people from both being deceived and becoming an instrument of deception in the lives of others.

Berth and Miriam Axlo, for example, were Swedish missionaries to Africa who are on Intercessors International's prayer list. Miriam was raised in southern Africa from the time she was two years old until she graduated from high school. She then returned to Sweden to attend Bible college, where she met Berth. After they married, the couple returned to Africa to continue the work Miriam's parents had begun there.

When an intercessor assigned to this missionary couple called with an urgent warning, suggesting they were about to receive poisoned meat, the staff at our headquarters prayerfully sought the Lord to confirm the legitimacy of the message. We all sensed individually that this word was from Him, so we contacted Berth and Miriam. They graciously received the word, though they certainly didn't understand it.

In the meantime, Berth and Miriam's adopted African daughter was to marry a young man who had just graduated from Bible school. In Botswana, the father of the groom is required to pay a "bride price" to the girl's parents, but this father refused. Berth needed the money to cover the expenses of the ceremony; so he visited the young man's father to address the matter. These parents were outraged that their son would marry a Christian, choose the bride without their permission and decide to serve the Lord. The father slaughtered a beast and offered it to ancestral spirits. He then offered the meat to Berth as a gift.

The memory of our recent phone call flashed through Berth's mind. Their daughter, not knowing of the message from the intercessor, exclaimed, "Don't take it! He has evil purposes!"

Several months later the father of the groom stood in church to give a false testimony. Just like Ananias and Sapphira who lied to God (see Acts 5:1-11), the man dropped dead on the spot!

In this case, the Lord used a personal intercessor to deliver Berth from death and deception. But many times the enemy will attempt to deceive God's children subtly through wrong thinking:

- The man is *deceived* if he is a hearer and not a *doer* of the Word of God (Jas. 1:22).
- He is *deceived* if he says he has no sin (1 John 1:8).
- He is *deceived* when he thinks himself to be "something" when he is nothing (Gal. 6:3).
- He is *deceived* when he thinks himself to be wise with the wisdom of this world (1 Cor. 3:18).
- He is *deceived* by seeming to be religious, when an unbridled tongue reveals his true condition (Jas. 1:26).

- He is *deceived*, if he thinks he will sow, and not reap what he sows (Gal. 6:7).
- He is *deceived*, if he thinks the unrighteous will inherit the kingdom of God (1 Cor. 6:9).
- He is *deceived*, if he thinks that contact with sin will not have its effect upon him.[1]

The enemy will use human reasoning whenever he can to deceive us from fulfilling God's plan. That is why we all need the prayers of a personal intercessor. In Genesis 2, God said, "From any tree of the garden you may eat freely; but from the tree of the knowledge of good and evil you shall not eat, for in the day that you eat from it you shall surely die" (vv. 16,17). By the time we read Genesis 3:6, the enemy is reasoning with Eve about the fact that the fruit from that tree is good for food, it looks appealing and it will make her wise. Human reasoning led to destruction then, and it still does!

Shortly after proclaiming Jesus to be the Messiah and learning that He would have to die on the cross, Peter tried to protect Jesus by saying, "God forbid it, Lord! This shall never happen to You" (Matt. 16:22). Peter loved Jesus and wanted to shield Him from pain. But Jesus rebuked Peter for that ungodly counsel, saying, "Get behind Me, Satan! You are a stumbling block to Me; for you are not setting your mind on God's interests, but man's" (v. 23). Human reasoning is an open door to deception.

Even the people who love us most can be used by the enemy to prevent us from doing a hard thing though it may be the right thing. Therefore, it is imperative that personal intercessors do not cloud God's truths with their own opinions. People need to hear what God thinks, not what human reasoning says (see Prov. 3:5,6; Ps. 108:12,13; 118:8,9). If someone calls you as a personal intercessor for advice, lift that person up in prayer and only speak if God releases you to do so.

Recognize the Seasons

You may be called upon to pray for someone for just a short while, or the Lord may ask you to intercede for that person for years. Only God can determine the length of the seasons of personal intercession. The point is that when the season ends, let it go without any feelings of guilt or condemnation.

When Tommi received news that her son-in-law had been brutally murdered, I (Beth) prayerfully rushed to her daughter, Carri's, side. Though Tommi normally has a very strong prayer life, I knew that surviving this trauma would take everything she had. For more than a year, I interceded as if I were Carri's mother.

I sat beside this beautiful young woman during court hearings and prayed for God's truth. I wept and wept for her. I read the Word over her picture, which I affixed to the front of my Bible. I called out for wisdom, knowledge and understanding on her behalf. I pleaded for protection from deception and trusted God to move the mountain of resistance out of her path. When the trial over the life insurance ended, the burden left and I suddenly realized I was no longer grieving or bearing the weight of Carri's pain in prayer. The grace covering had lifted and the season of personal intercession had ended.

Pitfalls of Personal Intercessors

Guilt when a season of intercession ends is only one of the pitfalls that personal intercessors face. Other temptations include:

- Bragging about the person(s) for whom they intercede

- Seeking that person's approval
- Sharing confidences under the guise of achieving the "prayer of agreement"
- Giving words at inappropriate times
- Using their own words as a ministry of correction
- Thinking so highly of the person that they neglect to speak truth into that individual's life
- Interpreting the words and visions received for others with their own understanding
- Fearing disapproval for giving a word that doesn't make sense

The Importance of Personal Intercessors

The anointing of the personal intercessor is always paired with another kind of anointing. They do not necessarily pray every day for the person(s) God has assigned to them unless their prayer-power mix is combined with the list anointing. Many personal intercessors, however, pray on a regular basis as the Holy Spirit brings that person to mind.

If the Lord has instructed you to intercede for someone, record what the Holy Spirit speaks to you. The Lord may give you a Scripture, an impression, a dream, a warning, a song or a word for that person. If so, write it down and wait for the Lord to show you how to follow through on it. As a personal intercessor, you will find that the more the Lord can trust you with, the more He will entrust to you. Personal intercessors have been known to change history by partnering in the lives of others. Let's look at the story of Esther as one example.

Mordecai, Esther's Personal Intercessor

When Mordecai adopted his orphaned niece, Esther, God called him to stand in the gap for her spiritually. Then, as God moved this radiant young virgin from the home of her loving uncle into the palace of King Ahasuerus, Mordecai began to intercede on her behalf. Daily he was seen pacing at the royal gates (see Esther 2:11) and would often have messages relayed to her. Because Esther had learned to trust God and wait for His timing, she was also aware of the gift she had received in Mordecai.

Esther deferred to the wisdom, knowledge and understanding of God shared through her uncle Mordecai, her personal intercessor. She relied on his intercession in conjunction with her own prayers to determine God's timing for sharing her Jewish heritage with her husband, King Ahasuerus. Together she and Mordecai waited upon God for a plan to reveal the sinister Haman's plot to destroy the Jewish people (see 3:6). Their unity and focus in prayer resulted in the miraculous. Esther was set free from the fear of what people might think of her. She was also catapulted into her destiny—saving the Jews of ancient Persia from utter destruction—when her husband, who deeply loved her, gave her a voice to speak into his empire. Esther transcended a life of obscurity and has been honored throughout the ages by the King of kings. To this day, she is celebrated through the feast of Purim.

And what about her personal intercessor, Mordecai? Because he partnered with God in prayer for Esther, Mordecai's humility was openly rewarded with praise, position and promotion. He became prime minister and received a double portion of joy: first, in seeing Esther's victory; second, in experiencing his own. One of the main lessons we see in Mordecai's personal intercession is that when we lay down our lives in prayer for others, God takes notice! The following list contains other instructive nuggets we have mined from Mordecai's example. We suggest that you read through the book of Esther to see what God says to you.

- Make sure your heart matches your actions with godly integrity.
- Pursue personal holiness so that your intercession can reflect the true heart of God.
- Determine that you will be submitted to authority so that you can qualify to speak with authority in the lives of those you guard in prayer.
- Let the prayer needs of others become the focus of your intercession.
- Ask God to give you His love for the person(s) you guard in prayer.
- Refuse to seek prominence or favor as you are called upon to deliver God's messages.
- Be a covenant keeper so that those who are relying on your intercession can trust in your loyalty, commitment and love.
- Invest quality prayer time, listening carefully to God's warnings and making sure that what you say does not conflict with His Word.
- Lay down all human reasoning so that you can receive the mind of Christ.
- Let the greatness of God rather than the magnitude of the problem motivate your boldness in intercession.
- Refuse to lie, even if you think it will vindicate God when He hasn't moved according to your timetable.
- Remember that the right word at the wrong time can thwart God's purposes, so don't speak unless or until you are sure you should.

- Realize that God's answers can take time, but persistence will either bring the desired result or a change in the way you view the request.
- Focus on the importance and greatness of God so that you won't be awestruck by the power and position of people.
- Don't be surprised by Satan's attempts to hang you for your effective intercession, but ask God to reveal a protective plan of redemption.
- If you are falsely accused, trust God to expose the matter and do not defend, gossip or retaliate.
- Believe that God has recorded His plans for your future and they are for good, not evil.
- Allow God to determine the reward for your intercession, knowing that He gives His best to those who leave the choice to Him.

Mordecai selflessly laid down his life to usher in God's enormous plan through another. He buried his own reputation to carry God's honor. He expected nothing but received everything.

This is the reality of personal intercession: It may require more than you ever expected to give, but it will always return more than you ever expected to get!

—————— **PERSONAL REFLECTION** ——————

Are You a Personal Intercessor?

1. Do people often seek you out to confide their personal prayer needs?
2. Is God repeatedly bringing one or two particular people to mind during your prayer time?

3. Has the Lord given you special insight about someone in order to pray for that person?

4. Would you rather pray for individuals or for the masses? If your answer is individuals, your prayer anointing includes that of a personal intercessor.

Note

1. Jessie Penn-Lewis, *War on the Saints* (New York: Thomas E. Lowe, Ltd., 1973), p. 11.

CHAPTER 5

FINANCIAL INTERCESSORS

FAITH FOR FUNDING

During the early 1800s, God apprehended a well-educated young Prussian playboy who was notorious for conning people and stealing their money. The son of a pastor, this handsome prodigal even went to jail before his father's prayers were finally answered. Shortly after his conversion, George Müller moved to London and learned of a wealthy dentist who believed that the Bible was to be taken literally. Anthony Norris Groves had given up his practice and all of his earthly goods to serve the Lord. When Dr. Groves wrote, "It ill becomes the servant to seek to be rich, and great, and honoured in that world, where his Lord was poor, and mean, and despised,"[1] George Müller surrendered everything to the Lord. His journal entry states:

> Honour, pleasure, money, my physical powers, my mental powers, all was laid down at the feet of Jesus, and I became a great lover of the Word of God. I found my all in God.[2]

George Müller became one of God's greatest financial intercessors. His purification toward money resulted in financial
power. Throughout his lifetime, he refused to ask or even tell
another human being about the material needs of the many
orphanages and schools he founded and administrated in
England. Every need was met through prayer.

Finding the Faithful for Funding

For some, the term "financial intercessor" conjures up a picture
of money moguldom. That thinking is simply not true. These
intercessors have been anointed by God to line up under heav-
en's financial corridors to summon funds on behalf of others.
The anointing to believe for large amounts of money is not to be
confused with the gift of giving, which does require resources.
The amount of money financial intercessors have is irrelevant;
these people are rich in faith for financial miracles for others.
God will, however, use the prayers of financial intercessors to
impassion the hearts of those who do have the gift of giving. At
times, the heavenly Father will even anoint them to pray in ideas
that promote prosperity. He also partners in their prayers to protect the finances of others.

God's Word tells us that Satan seeks to "steal, and kill, and
destroy" (John 10:10) the body, soul and spirit of each one of us
in order to prevent the gospel from being sent to and received by
the lost. One way he seeks to extinguish us is by imploding our
individual and corporate financial structures so that we will not
be able to underwrite the ministries that need our help. If he
cannot succeed in victimizing our businesses, he then attempts
to infect our minds with a lust for materialism or afflict our

bodies so that our finances will be funneled into preserving our physical frames rather than building up Christ's Body, the Church. His ruthless assaults against the Church are one of the reasons God has raised up financial intercessors.

These intercessors commonly see the blockage preventing a financial breakthrough. For example, a financial intercessor was awakened during the night with the name of a person who was "on the take" in a worldwide ministry. Understandably, the founder of this ministry was questioning why God had forced him to take a spin at Job's wheel of misfortune. He was well acquainted with Proverbs 10:22, which assures us that godly wealth is money without trouble. He began to wonder what he was doing wrong and eventually lost his joy. Then, when the extortionist was exposed, the ministry again prospered and this leader saw the need to enlist the help of financial intercessors on his staff.

Psalm 1 exhorts us to seek only godly counsel. Unholy alliances will circumvent God's prosperity and may even cause our demise. This is one of the reasons that Intercessors International trains resource managers and other financial intercessors to stand in the gap for leaders. We pray for protection from "plants" by the enemy within the ministries and businesses we cover in prayer.

Planted to Perpetuate God's Glory

Though the devil may attempt to plant his delegates in the camps of the godly, the Lord, through prayer, will usually expose them and sometimes even redeem their lives for financial service. George Müller, for example, often stole from his father's parish before he surrendered to Christ. When we truly love God, we discover that He does not give wealth to perpetuate greed; He gives it to promote His kingdom on Earth. Someone once said that the last thing to be saved in most of our lives is our wallets. But when we've been through the financial refining fire and our motives for money have been purified, there is no good thing that He will withhold from us.

*W*hen we truly love God, we discover that He does not give wealth to perpetuate greed; He gives it to promote His Kingdom on earth.

Sometimes God raises up financial intercessors to give them supernatural ideas. The Kraft Foods company began with a desire to perpetuate the gospel. Chocolate lovers are aware that Hershey started with a desire to sweeten the lives of abused and orphaned children. Welch's developed a grape juice that is used in Communion services globally. Its Christian roots sprouted from a desire to send missionaries overseas. Sam Tam, author of the book *God Owns My Business*, began his work with a desire to glorify the Lord. He became one of the only people in the world to legally deed a $40 million business over to God.

Norman Grubb's incredible book *Rees Howells Intercessor* bears witness to God's enormous ability to provide when our only reason for prospering is to glorify the Father. Rees lived a life of total dependence upon the Holy Spirit in prayer. He willingly sacrificed all of his resources to obey the voice of God. The result was that he became a channel for enormous amounts of money. The Lord entrusted to his care much land and even mansions that were used to educate Christians and harbor the Jews. As the wealthy R. G. LeTourneau said, "It's not how much of *my* money that I give to God that counts. It's how much of *His* money I keep for myself."[3] Financial intercessors recognize that it ALL belongs to Father God. Those whose motives have been purified have no problem asking the Lord to finance heaven's plans upon the earth.

A Channel of Blessing

In the early '70s, I (Beth) asked the Lord to make me a channel of financial blessing for others. My thinking was, *"God, make me really rich and then I will give You at least 10 percent! I want to have lots of money so I can give it away."* At that time, I was praying for an American evangelist who was struggling to make ends meet. Then, not even a week later, I received a call: "Beth, I want to anonymously donate $200,000 to a ministry. If I give you a cashier's check for that amount, would you deliver it?" I was thrilled to be a part of that miracle. The phone calls continued to pour in. Within three days I had distributed $256,000 to other ministries, while Floyd and I barely had enough food to put on our own table.

I wrestled in prayer: "Father, we are scraping and striving to feed our family and yet You continue to send huge sums to others through us." I think I was probably a little confused at that point. Remember, I had expected Him to make me rich before I gave to others!

As I sat reverently before the Lord, I heard Him say, "Beth, you asked to be used as a channel. I have answered your prayer."

In reflection, I now see that those times of financial dependence upon the Lord laid the foundation for the purification, trust and relinquishment I would need as a financial intercessor for the leaders I intercede for today.

I (Karen) have also seen some incredible miracles as I have believed God to supply funds for myself and others. I now realize that it takes no more faith to believe for a small sum than it does to believe for a large amount. The question is: If it's all God's money, what does He want to do with it?

Not long ago, a friend invited me to a conference in Arrowhead Springs, California. I was excited to go, but realized I had been carrying around more than a few hundred dollars of God's offering money and didn't know where He wanted me to plant it. I spent some time with the Lord and heard Him say that I was to make the check out to Youth With A Mission (YWAM). I then asked Him if I should mail it to a couple I know who are part of that ministry. His reply startled me: "Make the check out and put it in your wallet. I will show you who to give it to at the conference."

Though I only knew the friend who invited me, I believed God would introduce me to someone from YWAM when I arrived. Nothing happened. Then, just before the conference ended, a precious young girl went forward to testify that she had recently accepted Christ and was believing God for the money to go on her first YWAM outreach. Can you guess how much money she needed? That's right! And I had the check all made out for her airfare. God delights to meet the needs of His children.

As a matter of fact, not long ago, Dennis and I began to experience a financial struggle of our own. Because I have long believed that if you need something, you must give that very thing away, I took one-third of the money I received for an editing job and planted it into God's kingdom. Just two weeks later I received a call from my former bank. They had discovered a $3,000 balance that had been untouched for more than 15 years. I was excited but knew it was not enough to bail us out of our pending need. So I took one-third of the $3,000 and planted it into another ministry. Now listen to this . . . an unexpected source sent us a check for $6,000! Praise be to God who gives more than we can ever hope or imagine!

DEPENDING UPON GOD

The Lord has asked many of His people to live by faith as the gift of giving is released to them through others. These people need to surround themselves with financial intercessors. Billie Boatwright, who often travels with the Intercessors International's teaching team, is a person who lives by faith. Before departing for India, Billie was short of funds. When she prayed about canceling the trip, the Lord told her to write the checks to pay her bills and trust Him for the money to cover them. This was a real leap of faith for her because she is so conservative. But knowing fully that she had heard the Lord's voice, Billie obeyed. Financial intercessors prayed. When she arrived at the post office and opened her rental box, she found a check large enough to not only cover the bills but to also provide some spending money. Rejoicing, she lifted her heart to God in praise and slipped the bills into the mail drop. Though God does not want us to be reckless in our spending, He does want to be extravagant in His love toward us.

I (Beth) learned about God's extravagant love during a sabbatical in 1995. I had been seeking my heavenly Father about a financial matter when He said, "Elizabeth, with ministers and money I am not well pleased." As a minister, I knew I was included in that category. I pondered the thought for a moment and heard Him say, "With ministries and money I am not pleased."

My response was, "Lord, I don't understand." Pointing to all the people I knew who had done so much for the Kingdom, I began to repent for any sins we had committed. As I lay on my face before Him, I asked for clarification.

His answer was life-changing: "My people make a budget and then ask Me to bless it. Why don't you ask Me how much I want to supply and then trust Me for that amount?"

Shortly after that encounter, I shared the experience with Tommi and we both repented. Prior to leaving for Dresden, Germany (in the eastern part of that nation), to teach a prayer seminar, the Lord began to speak to Tommi about charging a registration fee. Though I believed she had heard from the Lord, I questioned Him. After all these spiritual sojourners had been through, I simply could not understand why He would ask them to pay. Before long, the Father began to rebuke me, saying, "Beth, I do not want this to be a Third World country. I want to maintain the dignity of My people in this place. It must cost them something."

Later, when Tommi, Martina Wagner (Director of WAM, Intercessors International ministry in Germany) and I began to pray about what the Father wanted us to teach, the Lord reminded me, "Elizabeth, you have not asked Me how much I want to supply." The three of us united in prayer for an amount.

There was no question about the figure the Father had given me. I picked up a pen and inscribed the amount on the palm of my hand but did not share that number with the others. Tommi and Martina wrote their figures on separate slips of paper, but Martina began subtracting for moneys already collected from her total. When the three of us compared our numbers, they were the same—20,000 German marks, which was the equivalent of $17,000 in American money.

Martina began to cry, saying that though the amount she had received was 20,000 marks, she had deducted the registration and other moneys from it because these were such poor people. With only 123 intercessors in attendance, she could not imagine how God could meet that number. Actually, we all wondered!

Financial Worship

As we persisted in prayer, the Lord said, "Elizabeth, I want you to teach the people how to worship Me with their tithes and offerings." Once again I struggled because I had never done that before. I was, however, familiar with the Bible and knew that God brought His people together for two reasons: offerings and worship. I believed He was now calling for worship *with* offerings.

That day as I stood before the group, I said, "Tomorrow we will worship the Lord with our offerings. No one is to come empty-handed. I don't care how little you have, you are to bring what God places on your heart. Maybe that will be a slip of paper indicating something He is asking you to surrender, such as a gift or talent. It could be that He will ask you to give up a possession or release one of your children to Him. Only God can tell you what to give, but do not come without an offering."

The following day, I asked the group if they had brought their offerings. Everyone cheerfully responded. But the radiance upon the face of a 90-year-old woman, who stretched forth her weather-beaten hand to display the few pfennig she had gathered, will forever be emblazoned in my memory. We worshiped the Lord with only one song before I reminded the people that the offering was not to be given to Intercessors International but as worship to God.

I asked everyone to lift their offering up to the Lord and to pray over it. I then explained that many offering plates would be distributed, allowing each person to worship the Father with the sacrifice he or she was surrendering to Him. "Feel free to kneel or dance or do whatever the Lord calls you to do," I said, "but make sure you worship Him with it." The response was incredible! It took almost two hours to collect the offering. Some people were weeping and lying on the floor. Many knelt at the altar. Others were dancing with the plates over their heads. One elderly couple waltzed with the plate between them. I knew that the Father was well pleased.

When the offering was finally collected, it consisted of 19,500 German marks, one peacock feather, many slips of paper and eight buttons. I asked the pastor to explain the significance of the buttons. He stated that they had probably been given by someone old because the very poor were accustomed to sewing coins on their apparel as buttons and cutting them off when everything else had been spent. I glanced up and saw an old woman with a tattered, buttonless sweater and realized that she was the one. Then, with predictable grace, God sent another woman forward with a brand-new sweater that she was to give away. It fit that elderly lady perfectly. No matter what our age, we cannot outgive our heavenly Father, because He loves a cheerful giver!

Before I told the people how much we had believed God for, I announced the financial total of 19,500 marks. A stunned silence fell over the congregation. Suddenly, one of the pastors jumped to his feet and said, "No, no, sister Beth! It's 20,000!

God told us that the church is to reimburse the 500 marks you paid to rent the building!" The final amount was 20,000 marks— exactly what we had believed for!

I could not help but compare my feelings about this offering given by the 123 believers worshiping in what was once the Iron Curtain, with the offering that David took in 1 Chronicles 29:

> O LORD our God, all this abundance that we have pro- vided to build Thee a house for Thy holy name, it is from Thy hand, and all is Thine. Since I know, O my God, that Thou triest the heart and delightest in uprightness, I, in the integrity of my heart, have willing- ly offered all these things; so now with joy I have seen Thy people, who are present here, make their offerings willingly to Thee (vv. 16,17).

It is true that God is not a respecter of persons, but He is a respecter of integrity, sacrifice and faith!

When Financial Intercessors Meet Corporately

Now that we at Intercessors International have grasped a clear understanding of God's grace to anoint some intercessors with the faith to pray for finances, we carefully select those who will pray for the offering. When I (Tommi) arrived at a church in Switzerland to train a group of 120 intercessors in how to pray for the EXPLO 2000 conference, I learned that director HansPeter Nüesch of Campus for Christ Switzerland was there to share his vision. He still needed either 1 million additional Swiss franks or more registrations to break even on the EXPLO conference. Following HansPeter's presentation, the national prayer chairman for EXPLO wanted to take an offering. I suggested we wait until the financial intercessors had been identified.

After teaching on the various prayer anointings, the group was ready to apply the principles. I called all the financial intercessors to the front to ask Father God how much He wanted to provide in the offering. The other intercessors were to pray that the financial intercessors would hear clearly and have the faith to believe for that amount. I then asked the financial intercessors to set their faith in agreement with the Lord for that sum. Next, they were to pray that the other intercessors would hear the amount they were to give and be obedient to the voice of the Lord.

"*Whatever* the highest amount is, double it; because God always wants to do more than we expect"

We all prayed that the gift of financial giving would be released and that people would worship the Lord with their finances. The buckets were passed and we broke for lunch. During the break the offering was counted.

When we returned from our lunch, I called the financial intercessors forward again to share the amounts they were believing for in faith. Their answers ranged from 7,000 to 50,000 Swiss francs. One intercessor insisted, "Whatever the highest amount is, double it, because God always wants to do more than we expect!" We all shouted with praise when the total was finally announced—105,000 Swiss franks, which converts to about $70,000! This was by far the largest offering I had ever taken, and HansPeter was overwhelmed. God is faithful!

Pitfalls of Financial Intercessors

Faith is a key to financial intercession, and the Lord has promised that if we believe His prophets, we will prosper (see 2 Chron. 20:20). Often, however, a financial intercessor will erroneously think that he or she must engineer a plan for harvesting the amount needed. We have seen some financial intercessors who have encumbered themselves with debt because God did not release the funds they had hoped He would supply. Let's look at some of the other pitfalls these intercessors must overcome:

- Thinking that you have to be rich to believe for great amounts of money for others
- Condemning and doubting self while taking on the responsibility and pain for meeting the debt, when only God can supply the need
- Attempting to manipulate God through works when He does not deliver in accordance with your timing
- Refusing to allow God to purify the motives of the recipient before the funds are released
- Sharing with doubters who water down your faith
- Encouraging others to make pledges based on emotion rather than on the basis of what God has dictated

- Freezing with fear when the Lord calls you to become a channel for an amount of money or an idea that is bigger than you ever thought you could believe for

Joseph, God's Financial Intercessor

When God calls a financial intercessor to become part of a big plan, that person can expect to meet with obstacles and see the promise deferred. Proverbs 13:12 *(NIV)* says that "hope deferred makes the heart sick, but a longing fulfilled is a tree of life." Jacob's son Joseph was a financial intercessor with the faith to believe God for huge plans (see Gen. 37—41). That faith was birthed when he was a mere teen, but it wasn't brought to maturity without great testing. Through times of sorrow and delay, he grew in his ability to hear God's voice and put his trust in God alone. After many years of "hope deferred," Joseph became a tree of life both to the enemies in his family and to the nation that would one day hold his people in bondage.

Tucked within Joseph's story are countless morsels of wisdom for financial intercessors to chew on:

- Ask God for a vision, a plan or an amount to believe for so you can be used by God rather than strive to be blessed by Him.
- Wait to share the vision until the Lord releases you to do so.
- Never share God's plan with those who do not have His interests at heart.
- Expect God's promises to be delayed and assaulted.
- Realize that man's rejection is often God's protection.

- Do not take it personally when others become jealous.
- Bless your enemies, realizing that what your enemy means for evil, God will use to prosper you.
- Understand that people may neglect their promises, but God will never forget.
- Refuse to grumble, gripe, gossip or give up.
- Focus on the heart of God rather than on the hand of God.
- Develop a love for His Word, and believe it.
- Allow God to purify your motives.
- Ask the Lord to remove all fear of man and love of the world's wealth.
- Trust the Lord's timing even when circumstances look hopeless.
- Ask God for a discerning heart.
- Believe that God wants you to hear His secrets so that others can be prospered through you.
- Give yourself a break by striving for excellence, not perfection.
- Realize that whether you are in a prison or a palace, God can still use you.
- Expect God to align the right people and the right circumstances to fulfill His promises.
- Believe for greatness and avoid small thinking.

In believing God for a plan to prosper the pharaoh's empire, Joseph was also blessed. God's financial intercessors are called to be rich in faith for funding the dreams of others. In being obedient to that call, they often realize the fulfillment of their own dreams. Are you a spiritual Joseph? Be generous with your faith, and remember: "The generous man will be prosperous, and he who waters [others who are financially dry] will himself be watered" (Prov. 11:25).

Why not cast your prayers for someone else's funds upon the water and see what washes back upon the shores for you?!

PERSONAL REFLECTION

Are You a Financial Intercessor?

1. Do you have bold faith to believe God for large amounts of money?
2. Do you carry a burden for the financial needs of others?
3. Do you get excited about seeing individuals, groups or organizations prosper?
4. Does God ever give you dreams or visions that would further His kingdom?
5. Has He ever used you to network others for financial prosperity?

Notes
1. Roger Steer, *George Müller* (Wheaton, IL: Harold Shaw Publishers, 1981), p. 32.
2. Ibid.
3. Loren Cunningham, *Winning God's Way* (Seattle: Frontline Communications, 1988), pp. 37, 38.

CHAPTER 6

MERCY INTERCESSORS

∞

GOOD NEIGHBORS OF PRAYER

The media pummels us with stories of school shootings, gang violence and abuses of both personal and political power. We talk about one person's lack of mercy toward another as if this disregard for others were a new thing. Not so! Attitudes about people have actually changed very little since Jesus walked among us. In Luke 10, Jesus describes the three kinds of people that lived in His day—the same three kinds we interact with now. Let's read the story together from the *New Living Translation*:

> A Jewish man was traveling on a trip from Jerusalem to Jericho, and he was attacked by bandits. They stripped him of his clothes and money, beat him up, and left him half dead beside the road.
>
> By chance a Jewish priest came along; but when he saw the man lying there, he crossed to the other side of the road and passed him by. A Temple assistant walked

over and looked at him lying there, but he also passed by
on the other side.

Then a despised Samaritan came along, and when he
saw the man, he felt deep pity. Kneeling beside him, the
Samaritan soothed his wounds with medicine and band-
aged them. Then he put the man on his own donkey and
took him to an inn, where he took care of him. The next
day he handed the innkeeper two pieces of silver and
told him to take care of the man. "If his bill runs higher
than that," he said, "I'll pay the difference the next time
I am here."

"Now which of these three would you say was a
neighbor to the man who was attacked by bandits?"
Jesus asked.

The man replied, "The one who showed him mercy."

Then Jesus said, "Yes, now go and do the same" (vv.
30-37).

Each one of us, at one time or another, has fit into all three
categories of people described in Luke 10:

- We have all beaten someone up and needed God's
  mercy.
- We have all passed someone up who needed our mercy.
- We have all lifted someone up who needed both God's
  and our mercy.

Mercy intercessors, however, are the good neighbors of
prayer, who travel the highways of the hurting, looking for
someone to lift up. They are God's living stethoscopes. They do
not regard the outward appearance but instead hear the root of
a person's pain in order to extend the mercy of God to that root.

When lined up with their anointing, mercy intercessors are as able to weep for their enemies as they are for their friends because they have a "Cross"-eyed view of all God's creation. They see the need for forgiveness rather than judgment and are often chided for ministering to the wrong people. Windows of pain become window panes of opportunity for showing God's mercy as these intercessors identify with the hurts of both those who have been beaten and those who have done the beating.

A Mother of Mercy

No other human being in the twentieth century exemplifies a mercy intercessor better than Agnes Bojaxhiu. Born of wealthy parents and Albanian heritage in the small town of Skopje in Kosovo, Agnes learned to care for the poor by observing her mother's acts of sacrificial service. Being the progeny of a heroic father, who as a city councilman courageously laid down his life to take a stand against the Yugoslavian Communists, she learned to champion truth.

Though called to the mission field at age 12, Agnes did not fully pursue her life as a nun until she was 18. Giving up her own name as a sign of detachment from the world, Agnes took on the name of St. Thérèse of Lisieux, recognized by Catholics as the "Patron of the Missions." More than anything, Agnes, now Sister Teresa, wanted to "devote herself with blind obedience, and to serve Jesus, her spouse, with total love."[1]

In his outstanding biography *Teresa of the Poor*, Renzo Allegri shares his interviews with Mother Teresa—a woman who saw Jesus as her husband and all the hurting people of this world as their children. She believed her role was to care for her Spouse's children by praying, living and serving among the poor. Allegri says, "It did not matter to her that the person was a saint or a criminal, an athlete or a leper, a person in power or a person in despair. To her, that person was a child of God for whose eternal salvation Jesus died on the cross."[2]

"A radical difference lies in the fact that the people we help are poor against their will while we are poor by free choice."

Mother Teresa's call to "tie a belt of love" around the poorest of the poor in Calcutta was preceded by 18 years of delays and detours—many in the church were even jealous of her. But she remained undaunted by her foes and invested those years in preparation and prayer, meeting every opposing force with mercy. By showering her opposition with mercy, Mother Teresa also received mercy. Her rivals often became channels of provision for her work. This mother of mercy believed that "to be able to understand and help those who have nothing, we have to live like them. A radical difference lies in the fact that the people we help are poor against their will while we are poor by free choice."[3]

Mercy intercessors make the choice to identify with the hurts and needs of others. Like Mother Teresa—who lived in a chicken shack so the poor could be housed in a place of comfort—these intercessors will surrender their own needs in prayer to cry out on behalf of the hurting.

You Don't Have to Be Poor to Be Hurt or Homeless

Sometimes the hurting are those who live in the wealthiest of homes. On one occasion when my husband Dennis and I (Karen) stayed in a suite at the Ritz Carlton Hotel in Laguna Niguel, California, I perched myself on the bed and began to praise the Lord for the privilege of sleeping in such opulence. I had never seen so much crown molding in one room! Suddenly I heard the inaudible voice of the Holy Spirit exhorting me: "Karen, can you imagine taking every cent you have and investing it in this hotel room?"

My response was, "Of course not, Lord; this is not my home. I am only staying here for three days!"

The Lord's reply changed my life: "That's right. And in terms of eternity, that is about how long a lifetime lasts—three days. I want you to minister to the homeless."

Certain that the Lord was calling me to the streets of skid row where California's broken are often scattered along the cement sidewalks in tattered blankets and weather-beaten bodies, I agreed to go. But the Lord interrupted me. "No, I want you to minister to ALL the homeless. You see, anyone who does not know Me will be eternally homeless." It was at that point that I agreed to speak for a ministry that brings in the lost, regardless of the part of society they represent.

As a speaker, nearly every time I mention the fact that Dennis and I have been involved in prison ministry, I have been approached by at least one person who has a loved one in prison. My heart grieves over the havoc Satan has ruthlessly waged against God's creation. When asked, we usually follow up with a visit to the prison to pray for that person's relative. I once smuggled a Bible into a top security prison with the help of a guard. God has His intercessors of mercy stationed everywhere—we need only ask for His help!

Tears of Identification

Mercy intercessors are those who are most often seen weeping. Tears, however, can be a little annoying to others who do not operate in this anointing. As a mercy intercessor, I (Karen) find my inability to restrain my tears quite embarrassing at times. My grandchildren chuckle at the fact that I cry over the nightly news and cannot rest over stories they tell me about their classmates. My times in prayer are often sobbing sessions, even when my own life is going well.

On a prayer journey to Romania to intercede over the injustices of the children there, I (Tommi) watched the tears of a mercy intercessor change the spiritual ground of a nation.

We entered a high-level-security city very late one night. Our team had prayed that the Lord would hide us from the enemy and that no one would see us coming in or going out. The Lord provided a dense blanket of fog, confirming to us our need to accomplish His work in that area. The driver who transported us to our quarters informed us that many Jews had been massacred in a particular cemetery there. We were thankful to have accumulated this information.

Since we had received so little advance notice about the trip, we did not have time to plan a complete prayer strategy or to cultivate a sense of unity as a team. I wondered how this would work. Then, just before we departed from America, I heard a new song by the group Curious? entitled "Did You Feel the Mountains

Tremble."[4] The chorus began to play repeatedly in my mind: "Songs that bring Your hope, songs that bring Your joy, dancers who dance upon injustice . . ." The Lord said, "This is your strategy."

I realized that God the Father was calling us to dance upon the injustices in Romania. I phoned the women who were to join our team and gave them each specific research assignments. We spent our first day combining that research, praying and coming together as a team. Billie Boatwright had collected geographical information about the land. Rhonni Greig had gathered data about the 140,000 mistreated and malnourished orphans there. Mary Napier brought songs for us to sing. And my husband, Ralph, came to impart the Father heart of God to the children. We even brought candy for them.

We dedicated one whole day to creating a battle plan and training the local people who would be working as part of our team. Our first stop would be the cemetery where the Jews had been brutally massacred. There we planned to have a time of confession and forgiveness. I asked that a Romanian come forward to confess the sins of her people for the massacre of the Jews. A young Romanian woman volunteered. Then I asked for someone of Jewish heritage to come forward to extend forgiveness to the Romanians. Two people of Jewish heritage on our team volunteered.

We finally piled into the vans and drove to the cemetery. The scene was much like the solemn opening from the movie *Schindler's List*. Can you picture it? We are all bundled up in our raincoats, walking in huddles under our little umbrellas. Dusk has just set in. The atmosphere is eerie. The caretaker opens the cemetery gates for us and we reverently approach the spot where hell itself has left its ugly imprint. Reading from a pillar on the site of the massacre, gut-wrenching words quicken us to the core: "This marks the spot where 63 Jews were killed and they made soap from their bodies. And written on the bars of soap: This soap was made from the fat of Jews."

As the reading commenced and we all began to pray, the young Romanian girl started to sob. Weeping and weeping, she began to confess the sins of her people to the two Jews on our team. While she prayed, she buried her head in her hands and cried out, "Oh, God, forgive us!" She was sobbing from the depths of her soul in repentance. She continued to wail with words of confession in her native tongue. We looked down and saw a puddle of blood about the size of a basketball imprint. The rain then caused the blood to spread out along the pavement. A team member turned to me. Our eyes locked. Together we just looked at each other and said, "Without shedding of blood there is no forgiveness" (see Heb. 9:22). Again we looked down—her hands were covered with blood. She had wept so hard that her nose bled profusely. She had shed blood.

My mind drifted back to a similar setting when Jesus the Savior of the world agonized in the garden, sweating drops of blood for a cruel and unrepentant world (see Luke 22:44). The sins of a nation toward God's people had once again compelled the heart of God to pour forth His mercy—this time through one of His intercessors. In our hearts we knew that mercy would one day bring healing to the anti-Semitic root in that land.

On the airplane I had picked up the September 1998 issue of *National Geographic* and read a story entitled "A Nation Savors Freedom: Romania's." The article provided graphic photos of neglected children living in squalor within the walls of ill-equipped state orphanages that had become dumping grounds for Romania's discarded kids. The following day we visited some of these orphanages. We were told we would not be allowed to touch the children. In preparation for our visit at one of the state orphanages, the place had been doused in bleach to cover the smell of urine. We almost passed out from the fumes. The children had been cleaned up for our benefit; however, they were still dirty according to American standards. We noticed that they had no toys and were enthralled by the presence of a mouse. We felt sorry for the mouse as they all webbed around it. Clearly, these children were desperate for love and attention. Ralph cradled many of them in his arms.

Billie confessed that she felt helpless. She was sure that visitors going into the orphanage to provide candy and leaving immediately afterward had only added to the sense of loneliness and rejection the children already felt. Billie and Rhonni, both mercy intercessors, left with tears streaming down their cheeks. As a matter of fact, that night Billie and Rhonni continued to weep for the children at regular intervals. At one point, they were simultaneously awakened by the sound of rustling beside their bed. Rhonni reached over and touched a stack of Romanian Bibles and toys she had brought for the orphans. They were wet! She crawled out of bed and moved them away from the window. The rustling continued. She flipped on the light to see if it was raining outside. The moon-splashed terrain was clearly dry. There was no evidence of water leaking anywhere. When Billie asked the Lord to reveal the source of the noise, He simply replied, "I am weeping with you."

On our last day in Romania, our dedicated team ventured into the center of town to pray that the hearts of the children would be restored to their fathers and that the fathers would be restored to their children. As we started to dance upon the injustices in that malignant place, the Lord anointed Mary with a prophetic song. I pivoted about and noticed that some little gypsy children had clustered around us. Children . . . out of nowhere God had sent children. We clutched hands and began to dance with them. We danced upon the injustices against the children in the land, with the children of the land. What an awesome sight to see God's heart of mercy poured out upon the land for His little ones. He had given us the strategy and then handpicked the children who were to perform it. The Lord truly has a heart of mercy for all the little children of the world!

Mercy, the Heart of Healing

Mercy intercessors are usually the first to enlist in hospital visitation programs because they cannot bear to see suffering without crying out for healing. When Pat Richardson's friend contracted cancer, she prayed and prayed for healing. Despite four months of constant prayer and laying on of hands, her close friend died, leaving two young children and a grief-stricken husband behind. That death provoked a season of deep depression and incredible spiritual doubt in Pat. She quit the hospital visitation program and said that if she had not been diligent in her daily Bible reading, her flame of passion for the Lord might have become a flickering wick.

The downward spiral of emptiness she experienced began to weaken not only her faith but also her physical body. When a neighbor and Christian friend took notice, she insisted that Pat accompany her on a daily walking regime. Eventually Pat began to reconnect with God and His Church Body. Nearly 14 months later, Pat's pastor called to ask her to go to the hospital and pray for a homeless lady who had attended the church only twice. Let's read the story in Pat's own words:

It was late and I really didn't want to go because the storm outside was so fierce. Pastor had told me that the lady was not expected to live many days and that she just needed someone to be by her side. I consented.

Carolyn was a 36-year-old alcoholic, weighing about 360 pounds and afflicted with pneumonia and cirrhosis of the liver. A liver transplant was not an option. When I first met her, she was thrashing with fear upon the bed. The weight of her body caused the bed to toss about the room. I had never seen anyone so overcome with fear.

I asked her if she was a Christian and she affirmed that she was. My first words to her were, "Why are you allowing Satan to do this to you? This is not the way God would want you to respond. You are called to be the righteousness of Jesus." Those words seemed to calm her.

For the next month, I went to the hospital daily to mentor Carolyn. I shared about God's character, His awesome forgiveness and His loving arms that were out-stretched toward her. God used me to teach Carolyn how to die; she found the peace of God. Before she left this earth, she had entered into His rest and was assured of His love for her.

God had not only used me to bless Carolyn, He had also used her to get me back on track with Him. Once again I began to read and apply Scriptures regarding healing. I finally realized that God *does* heal, but we can't manipulate Him to do so. I love to pray for healing and I believe God has anointed me for that, but I also know that the outcome of prayer is dependent upon the Lord and not me. Our heavenly Father—not I—determines when a person's assignment has been completed. He uses me to stop the premature removal of His people, and I must be faithful to pray to that end. It seems to me that when God anoints me to pray for healing, there is an inner knowing within me that the person prayed for will be healed. Perhaps it is a release of faith; I often "know that I know" when a healing is taking place.

I have changed my attitude about death. I now believe that when a person's assignment has been completed, death becomes "moving day." Christians don't die; they simply move from one home to another. His Word tells us that "precious in the sight of the LORD is the death of His godly ones" (Ps. 116:15). I know that I serve the God "who pardons all your iniquities; who heals all your diseases; who redeems your life from the pit; who crowns you with lovingkindness and compassion; who satisfies your years with good things" (Ps. 103:3-5). The Lord is mercy, and it is His mercy that causes our healing. I trust in His mercy.

WHY MERCY INTERCESSORS?

Mercy is usually accompanied with tears to cleanse and soften hard places. One of the most poignant verses in the entire Bible reports: "Jesus wept" (John 11:35). Jesus wept before He raised Lazarus from the dead. Why spill tears if the healing is certain? The answer to this question lies in the fact that when tears are released, an unleashing happens on three levels: spiritual, emotional and physical:

- Tears unleash the heart of God. They show our spiritual dependence upon the heavenly Father. They are the outward sign of our inward brokenness and need for Him (see Ps. 34:18; 51:7,8). Jesus' tears represented His identity with and dependence upon the Father's heart of mercy toward all who are broken.

- Tears unleash a spirit of identification. They demonstrate a heart connection with others. Romans 12:15 gives us the key to friendship: "Rejoice with those who rejoice, and weep with those who weep." Jesus' tears represented His identity with the hurts of people. He is a friend to all who call upon Him in truth.

- Tears unleash physical acts of healing. I (Karen) have been told by friends in the medical profession that tears actually create a physical change in our bodies, causing healing hormones to be released and some of the physical stress that is trapped within to be alleviated. Jesus' tears represented the release of a healing that was about to occur in the physical realm.

The Lord commonly uses mercy intercessors to release His heart over a people group, nation or issue. We find that as that happens, a physical demonstration of mercy will usually follow.

As a matter of fact, the body, soul and spirit are so closely connected that what happens in one realm will usually affect the others. We have found the same to be true in nations. What happens in the spiritual realm affects the land, and what affects the land affects the people there.

Mercy intercessors who also have an anointing to pray for nations can be the key to unlocking God's purposes in those places. When Beverly McIntyre heard about the 170,000 wounded during the Bosnian War—including thousands who were victims of sexual brutality—the 200,000 starved and killed, as well as the 35,000 maimed and injured children, and the 750,000 displaced people forced to leave their comfortable homes, she wept and prayed. Haunted by those disturbing facts, her mercy heart of intercession bore a weight that only God could have helped her carry. The Lord shared with Beverly the depth of His love for the people in that war-torn region of the world.

Eventually her prayers of mercy were translated into action. Accompanied by her husband and several other women with a call of God to help, Beverly founded a ministry called Change Point. Together she and her friends formed a Croatian team. The heavenly Father showed this team that before these war-ravaged women could receive Jesus, the true treasure of life, they would have to receive material gifts and know they had not been forgotten by His people. Beverly and her team began to load up their hearts with mercy and their arms with presents. They now minister to rape victims and shower them with God's love, both prayerfully and physically. As a result, they have seen many Muslim, Orthodox and Catholic women invite Jesus into their hearts.

First the prayer of identification with the vastness of the Father's heart, then the friendship of identification with others emotionally, and finally the identifying signs of healing or physical change in the natural—that is the cycle of mercy intercession!

Pitfalls of Mercy Intercessors

Identification is one of the significant strengths of the mercy intercessor's prayer profile; it can also be a hindrance. Let's explore the pitfalls that accompany this anointing:

- Rescuing—wanting so desperately to pad others from pain that they prevent God's hand of corrective discipline from accomplishing His purposes

- Acting naively about the enemy's tactics
- Being judged, mocked or quenched by others who feel uncomfortable with their tears
- Refusing to deliver a hard word because they don't want to hurt anyone
- Getting involved where God has not commissioned them
- Thinking that mercy intercession is not for men, even though most of the tears in the Bible are associated with men
- Grieving to the point of giving up their lives in despair rather than laying down their lives in prayer to plant seeds of hope and change
- Becoming angry with God when He allows others to suffer
- Feeling lonely, unappreciated and hurt when others don't hear a call to meet the needs of those for whom they have a heart to minister
- Judging those who do not operate within the same anointing
- Succumbing to manipulation during God's seasons of delay
- Identifying to the point of depression
- Refusing to let go when God's season for helping someone has ended

Jeremiah, the Prophet with a Mercy Intercessor's Anointing

Does it sound strange to you to hear land described with an ability to cry or to become bitter? Let's read from Lamentations 1:

How lonely sits the city that was full of people! She weeps bitterly in the night. The roads of Zion are in mourning. . . . And she herself is bitter (vv. 1,2,4).

In 931 B.C., Israel split into two kingdoms: the northern kingdom that maintained the name Israel and the southern kingdom that became known as Judah. The division of the land mirrored the divided hearts of God's people who refused to stay dependent upon Him. The similitude between the destruction of the land when it was split in two and the destruction of the people when they split in their devotion to God is uncanny.

Like Jesus who later wept over the city of Jerusalem (see Matt. 23:37; Luke 19:41), Jeremiah also lamented over the ruination of that city and the nation that had been created to cradle the peace of God within its borders. No other prophet in the Old Testament is more connected with tears than he.

Any quick glance at Jeremiah's biography bears witness to his anointing as a mercy intercessor and his identification not only with the land but also with the people who once occupied it. He pined over the wayward hearts of God's people. That mourning compelled his prophetic mission as he called the people to repentance. It seems that no matter how much Jeremiah wept, the people would not listen. No matter how much he grieved, God did not stop the destruction that resulted from their refusal to turn toward Him.

Jeremiah could see that because the people had sown to the wind, they were now reaping the consequences of their actions. What he did not focus on were God's acts of mercy in allowing those consequences to drive the people back to their place of safety in Him. The heavenly Father knew that by exchanging the God of flesh for a god of stone, their hearts would also turn to stone and would have to be crushed in order to be softened again.

The Lord poured His heart out to Jeremiah and allowed him to share in the suffering God felt over His wayward people. Though Jeremiah mediated between God and sinful humanity, the choice to turn them around was not his to make. Thus he dealt with unprofitable feelings of rejection and futility. Imagine how depressing it would have been to think that both God and His people have forsaken you for loving them. Sounds a lot like Jesus, doesn't it?!

Unlike Jesus, however, who bore rejection without striking out at self or others, Jeremiah provides a picture of our need for mercy even as we give it. Let's review some of the lessons from the lamentations of his life:

- Realize that tears are a gift of identification with God's heart toward people.
- Praise God for brokenness and believe that it will be used to carry a message of future blessedness.
- Take comfort in the fact that God puts more value on people than He does on possessions—and He can restore both.
- Accept God's assurance that "if He causes grief, then He will have compassion according to His abundant lovingkindness. For He does not afflict willingly, or grieve the sons of men" (Lam. 3:32,33).
- Surrender your right to control the outcome of another person's choice.
- Pray with a view from the Cross, knowing that even the enemies of your loved ones need God's mercy.
- Refuse to judge the motives of others.
- Do not take it personally when change doesn't occur in the time frame and way you had hoped.
- Believe in God's ability to alter the circumstances, no

matter how horrible they may appear.

- Do not quit praying with faith until God releases you to do so.
- Hope in God, not in people.
- Don't be desperate for answers; rather, surrender to His wisdom.
- Be discerning about the connection between the land and the people.
- Stay alert to the adversary's strategies to depress you and make you feel rejected.
- Pray for truth so that righteousness can be established.

In reaching out to others, mercy intercessors will usually find that they have settled in the shadow of the Almighty (see Ps. 91:1). And though shadows can feel like darkness, when God is in charge, they are messengers of protection. The shadow of His Hand often precedes the healing that flows from His heart.

Trust in His mercy!

—————— **PERSONAL REFLECTION** ——————

Are You a Mercy Intercessor?

1. Are you deeply grieved over issues that you know are breaking the heart of God?
2. Is it difficult for you to give a hard word for fear of hurting someone's feelings?
3. Do you struggle with or judge people who don't seem sensitive to the root of pain going on in the hearts of others?
4. Are you accused of being sensitive to the wrong people?

5. Do people find it easy to share their hurts with you?

6. When people share their pain with you, do you have difficulty letting it go?

Notes

1. Renzo Allegri, *Teresa of the Poor* (Ann Arbor, MI: Servant Publications, 1996), p. 39.

2. Ibid., p. 147.

3. Ibid., p. 131.

4. "Did You Feel the Mountains Tremble?" by Martin Smith, ©1994 Curious? Music, UK/PRS/ Admin. in North America by EMI Christian Music Publishing, Brentwood, TN.

5. "A Nation Savors Freedom: Romania's," *National Geographic* (September 1998), pp. 32-59.

CHAPTER 7

CRISIS INTERCESSORS

PARAMEDICS OF PRAYER

E-mail has made it easy to transmit urgent matters from one end of the earth to the other. In order to receive those messages, however, your computer must be turned on and you must be online if you want to make contact. Crisis intercessors are those who are online with God at all times. They are the paramedics of prayer, rushing in and out of the throne room with urgent requests *for* the Father and *from* the Father on behalf of others. When coupled with a spiritual warfare anointing, crisis intercessors are the watchmen who intercept and do battle with trespassers in the war between the kingdom of light and the kingdom of darkness.

I (Karen) have engraved in my memory the first time I spent a whole week with Beth Alves—her role model gave me complete understanding of the term "crisis intercessor." I quit counting the number of times I would be steeped in some trivia when God spoke to Beth about a pending need for one of the many leaders she is committed to in prayer. Beth's quickenings to pray are carried out on the spot! I've heard her say, "Delayed obedience is disobedience!" And she is the most obedient crisis intercessor I know. This woman is online day and night to guard God's leaders!

Up Close and Personal with the Father's Concerns

Crisis intercession is not only for leaders but also for healings, finances, family, nations or any other pending issue on the Father's heart. In her book *Becoming a Prayer Warrior*, Beth provides the backdrop for our portrait of a crisis intercessor. Let's read it together:

> I crawled out of bed in the middle of the night for a glass of water, when a picture of my cousin [whom I had not seen in 10 years] canvassed my mind. Suddenly I dropped to my knees and began to cry out, "God, don't let Mike move! Keep him still, Lord! Keep him still! Oh God, please don't let him move! Hold him, Lord. Hold him."
>
> Even though I was pleading on Mike's behalf with my words, I remember thinking, *This is ridiculous! Why am I praying this?* Then the words ceased, and when they did, I could not muster another word. So I got up, drank a glass of water and started toward the bedroom. Again I fell to the floor and began to cry out with a grave sense of urgency, "Don't let him move, God! Don't let Mike

move! Stay still! Stay still!" The words came to an abrupt end. This time I thought, *Oh no! This must be a nightmare!*

I had no feeling inside of me other than to pray. I got up and began to pray, wondering what in the world that was all about. One more time I took a few more steps toward the bedroom when again I dropped to the floor. Only this time I was yelling, "Get him up, Lord! Get him to run! Run, Mike! Lord, help him to run . . . run . . . run! Let him run, God! Run, run, run!" After several minutes, a calm came over me and I returned to bed for the night.

The following day I called my aunt to see if she could help me put the pieces together about my puzzling outcries the night before. She informed me that Mike was in Vietnam. The experience still made very little sense.

Finally, a month later, my aunt called to read a letter she had received. The letter told how Mike, who was a pilot, had been shot down and landed in a tree. He had been warned to get out of the area as quickly as possible but explained that just a few hundred yards from the crash site he fell into a bush. "Mom," he wrote, "it was like I was pinned down. I felt like somebody was sitting on me. The Vietcong came and were unknowingly standing on my pant leg while looking up at my parachute in the tree. They turned around and began to slash the bushes with their bayonets. It looked safe, so I started to get up and was about to run when once again I fell into the bush as though someone were pushing me. The Vietcong had returned. I laid there a couple of minutes and again had an impulse to get up and run. I heard a helicopter so I sprinted through a wooded area, following the direction of the noise, to an open space where I was whisked off to safety. The helicopter crew said they came in response to my beeper. And yet, my beeper was not working when I was shot down!"[1]

When Today's Timing Meets Tomorrow's Trouble

Although crisis intercessors are generally called to pray for problems occurring in the now, the Father may start the intercession today to ward off tomorrow's trouble. The following story by Chrystle White graphically illustrates the way God's time frame sometimes works:

> In 1965, during a family reunion in Florida, my grandmother woke everyone at 2:00 A.M., issuing orders to get empty Coke bottles, corks and paper. "I've received a message from God," she said. "People must hear His Word." She wrote verses on the paper while the grandchildren bottled and corked them. Then everyone deposited over 200 bottles into the surf at Cocoa Beach.
>
> People contacted and thanked my grandmother for the Scriptures throughout the years. She died in November 1974. The next month the last letter arrived:
>
> Dear Mrs. Gause,
>
> I'm writing this letter by candlelight. We no longer have electricity on the farm. My husband was killed in the fall when our tractor overturned. He left 11 young children and myself behind. The bank is foreclosing; there's one loaf of bread left; there's snow on the ground; Christmas is two weeks away. I prayed for forgiveness before I went down to drown myself. The river

has been frozen over for two weeks, so I didn't think it would take long. When I broke the ice, a Coke bottle floated up. I opened it, and with tears and trembling hands, I read about hope. Ecclesiastes 9:4, "But for him who is joined to all the living there is hope." Hebrews 7:19; 6:18 and John 3:3 were also referenced. I came home, read my Bible, and am thanking God. Please pray for us, but we're going to make it now. May God bless you and yours. —A farm in Ohio[2]

Nine years before her death, Mrs. Gause responded with prayer and action to a crisis that would save the life of a hopeless widow. Only the Lord understands the details of that Coke bottle's journey from a sand-swept beach in Florida to an ice-clad river in Ohio. He knows the precise moment our crisis intercession will pierce the heavenlies to become the life-changing prayers that will tip the prayer bowls in another person's life (see Rev. 5:8)! We need only be obedient, even when it doesn't make sense!

CRISIS INTERCESSORS AT CRISIS SITES

Our heavenly Father not only knows trouble's timing, but He also knows how to position crisis intercessors at just the right place to enable them to partner in prayer for the details. Seldom do these intercessors fully know why they are in "the" place until confronted with the need to intercede. The key is to stay prayerfully close to God. The following story vindicates God's ways of streamlining our steps to get us to our appointed stations of intercession, even when we can't understand why we are there. Anne Thompson tells it in her own words:

Two weeks ago I witnessed an accident at about 8:30 P.M. I arrived just seconds after a Suburban overturned and saw a young man thrown from the vehicle and lying on the opposite side of the highway in the middle of oncoming traffic. A yellow car traveling about 65 miles per hour hit him; he bounced in the air like a rag doll. Then another car hit his body. He bounced up again; another car followed.

The Scripture came to mind, "The steps of a good man are ordered by the LORD, and He delights in his way" [Ps. 37:23, *NKJV*]. I knew the Lord had ordered my steps, so I went into intercession immediately. The groaning in the Spirit was instantaneous. I couldn't believe what I had just seen!

I wondered about the families. Who were they? How could I tell them that I was there but could not stay at the scene of the accident for fear that bystanders might be killed in the darkness? I learned from the nightly news that the Suburban was transporting a group of kids from a local high school. My pain was almost unbearable.

Then, at last Sunday's service, the pastors and congregation prayed for a 20-year-old man named James, who was in the critical care unit at a local hospital. I went to visit him. Just as I was leaving, a man dressed in a suit, accompanied by his wife and two teenage sons, entered the unit. He introduced himself as a pastor who had simply heard that James was in a coma. After exchanging formalities, the pastor said, "I had a son killed two weeks ago."

I asked, "Was your son killed in a car accident near the speedway on Saturday night?" With shock and surprise, the pastor said, "Yes, how did you know?"

"I saw your son killed," I replied.

He begged me to share what I had seen, but I told

him the sight was too horrible to repeat. "No, no," he said. "Please tell me every detail. I need to know. I can handle it. Please." I began to share with him. He cried and I burst into tears. He held me in his arms as we both sobbed deep tears of grief.

I rehearsed the way God had ordered my steps that tragic night. I was there before anyone else arrived but didn't know why until that moment. God's eye had never left this man's child—not for one second! The Lord had positioned a crisis intercessor at that very instant for his son. His eye was indeed on the sparrow and I knew He was watching over him. I also knew He was watching over the family and why I had seen the accident.

This father desperately needed to know the details—the puzzle pieces of his son's death. As I gave them to him, his heart began to enter God's rest. He found closure in knowing the truth. The compassion of God was incredible. Together we saw the heart of the heavenly Father at work through crisis intercession.

The Warning of Crisis Intercession

The Lord may send a spiritual foreboding to warn His crisis intercessors about impending danger. This threat might begin as a sense of unrest or even inner turmoil. Or, it might start with a heart tug from the Holy Spirit to say or do something beyond the ordinary. Sometimes God will send a dream to root the message in our minds. We should remain on the alert, while remembering that even mature crisis intercessors can fail to recognize God's signals and obey them.

Speaking of signals, I (Beth) was in Reichlinghausen, Germany, officiating over the prayer ministry for a large prayer conference held in a soccer stadium there. Tommi was coleading. The event was progressing smoothly, but God had spoken to my heart before I left for Germany that I was to pray against the spirit of death. I had even asked my personal intercessors to intervene against death in accidents for Tommi and myself as well as our team members.

Even mature crisis intercessors can fail to recognize God's signals and obey them.

The concluding hour of the conference was underway and 10,000 teenagers were being commissioned into intercession. Some parents and leaders had already begun loading their tents and luggage into a car. People working behind the scenes were winding down. The doctor in charge of the first-aid room, Peter Reis, had closed up shop and had been thanking God for a fairly stressless event. Entrenched in deep concentration over the sermon he was preparing, he barely noticed little Petertje, his jovial 13-month-old son, playing on the nearby ground with some stones that had captivated his attention.

Suddenly, a blood-chilling shriek cut through the calm. Whipping his head into an upright position, Dr. Reis's eyes poised on the startled face of a chauffeur sitting in the driver's seat of a Citroën station car. The driver, emotionally paralyzed by the frenzied screams of bystanders, failed to identify the human bump that lay beneath him—little Petertje.

The right wheel had bulldozed over the boy's shoulder, back up to his pelvis and then forward again. Not knowing which way to turn, the floundering driver had stopped the car on Petertje's now mashed little head. Gasping in disbelief, Dr. Reis could only see his son's blond hair peeking out from beneath the tire. Someone motioned the chauffeur to move the car backward. A tire imprint across the boy's face bore witness to the trauma his vulnerable little body had sustained. Dr. Reis cradled the lifeless toddler in his arms and sighed, "My child is dead."

In the meantime, I was notified by walkie-talkie of a code blue for a little boy. I stepped up on the stage and addressed the speaker, who quickly summoned the crowd into service: "A little child has been run over. This is your first commission! We will be praying for a miracle!" A wave of prayer rose up with people praying in the languages of many nations.

Little Petertje's sister approached me, her face shrouded in despair. I knew I had to accompany her into a tent for privacy and minister faith to her. Like her father, she, too, was hopelessly convinced that a funeral would follow. I shared the testimony of a time when my own daughter was healed on her deathbed. "You must believe with me! You must have faith!" I insisted. She grabbed me tightly, sobbing in my arms. Finally, she choked out the words, "I'll believe if you'll believe with me." We nestled together in the tent, expecting the God of the Resurrection to bring forth a miracle. The kids outside were all praying in one accord. They prayed for 20 minutes until the groundswell of weeping and praying, weeping and praying gave vent to praise and thanksgiving.

Our 24-hour-prayer coverage was also continuing in the prayer room. Jean Krisle was the watch leader and began to war with the other intercessors against the spirit of death. The Lord gave them the assurance that little Petertje would live and not die. The joint anointings of crisis, mercy and spiritual warfare were now working together in one concerted prayer.

Our God Reigns

Petertje had been transported to the hospital and the family was awaiting the results of brain scans and X rays. But when a staff member finished examining the boy's head, she found that he was conspicuously normal. The only residue from the accident was a gash here and there. It was a miracle! God's people had rallied together in corporate prayer with focused faith and God had honored that faith!

The horror of seeing his son dead in his arms has now changed Dr. Reis's whole medical practice. As a general practitioner, he has become a powerful intercessor, especially for youth who are sick.

This child's story of resurrected life was broadcast on the secular news and recorded in a secular magazine. As I reflect on the incident, I often wonder what would have happened if God had not begun the process with a warning to His crisis intercessors. The spiritual ground had been prepared for protection long before the accident occurred, and others were aligned to "pray in" the miracle.

Pitfalls of Crisis Intercessors

Believing that you are in the right place for the right reason is a paramount challenge for crisis intercessors. It is common to sec-

ond-guess yourself, wondering if it's just your imagination compelling you to go or do or say something, or whether it really is
the Lord. Let's explore some of the other pitfalls that challenge
crisis intercessors:

- Feeling guilty for not responding when the opportunity to intercede is neglected
- Looking for a crisis in every situation
- Neglecting to use wisdom in corporate intercession,
  and instead interrupting with any idea or impression,
  rather than a true crisis
- Running on adrenaline from crisis to crisis instead of
  focused faith, and getting a druglike "high" from these
  crises
- Procrastinating or putting oneself in dangerous situations or time crunches and then "crashing" at the
  end
- Moving from crisis to crisis in prayer without spending time in a loving, intimate relationship with the
  Lord
- Refusing to release the situation because you don't
  see, hear and feel the results, even when the Holy Spirit
  has given an inner witness to do so
- Carrying guilt for life-and-death situations that are
  not manifested in victory
- Basking in the past and thereby missing the present
- Falling prey to the enemy's "if onlys" and accusations
  for not praying long enough or hard enough
- Accepting judgment from others when you have
  already prayed it through, received the peace of God
  and cannot muster up another prayer
- Taking on the burden personally

King David, God's Crisis Intercessor

The word "crisis" carries a call to answer the urgent cries of someone in peril. We think of those who rise up with heroism during crises as extraordinarily courageous, but many later admit that their acts have been born more out of instinct than valor. Not so with Jesse's son David, the shepherd boy who later became King David of the Old Testament. David intervened in accordance with God's heart and prayerfully rose to the occasion when God's people and kingdom were threatened. His courage reflected his ability to conquer a "man-pleasing" focus and to instead focus on what God was saying so that he would always be alert to trouble.

The Bible first spotlights David in action as a humble young boy fighting the Philistine superman of his day. Clothed in more than 150 pounds of man-made armor and driven by pride, the giant Goliath's duel with a slingshot-bearing David is almost laughable. But David is merely walking out a prayer strategy of crisis intercession when he cuts off the arrogant head of Goliath. Crisis intercession coupled with warfare can bring down trouble in one swift instant!

David, however, is about to learn that being the man of the hour in crisis intercession is not something to base your future on. Though it hardly seems fair, David's heroism makes him the target of jealousy by the very person he helped—King Saul. In godly fashion, David blesses his enemy whose hatred has now opened the door to the torment that usually accompanies unforgiveness and envy.

Remarkably, King Saul's tormenting outbursts become interventions of crisis intercession for David. Most of us know the story: David is forced to leave everything behind to survive the rage of the green-eyed monster driving King Saul. And yet, because David had trained his ear as a crisis intercessor, he is able to outrun and outsmart his enemy. The Lord awakens David with warnings of danger, alerts him through circumstances and people, and helps him to identify problems before they arise. Years of moving from crisis to crisis begin to build his character and teach him how to identify with hurting and rejected people. Though he is a man who knows how to fight, he also becomes a man of mercy and worship.

Crisis intercessors often share a similar prayer DNA—they have a desire to bring healing to those who are hurting. Like David, they must learn to lean upon God first—and not people—for strength and strategies (see Ps. 60:11; 108:12). Then, when their hearts have been fully knit to God's, He will generally raise up trustworthy friends who can confirm His messages in times of crisis intercession. For David, that friend was Jonathan.

God used Jonathan to keep David's hands strengthened, his heart aligned and his feet from stumbling into the enemy's traps. After Jonathan's death, David's life lacked the luster of faith, purity and prayer it had known when the two friends walked side by side. By being in the wrong place at the wrong time, David opened the door to lies, murder and adultery.

From this crisis intercessor we learn the importance of remaining close to God and close to His people. Only when we are in right relationship with God and others can we be sure that we are exactly where we belong and are hearing correctly from God. You can read David's story in the books of 1 and 2 Samuel. The following are other lessons to be gleaned from David's example:

- Listen before you leap and be alert to God's SOSs.
- Conquer your "fear of man" in order to hear and obey the strategies of the Lord.

- Be accountable in the ordinary if you want to be called upon for the extraordinary.
- Know that true crisis intercession flows out of an intimate love relationship with God, rather than from a service mentality.
- Allow humility to become your defense against pride by recognizing your complete dependence upon God.
- Make sure your motives have been submitted to the heavenly Father before you intervene in a crisis.
- Believe that the enemy's resources cannot compare with God's power: Five stones are superior to a sword when God is in charge!
- Give more credence to your spiritual armor than to your physical strength.
- Know that you will not always be appreciated and sometimes you will even be jealously despised when God uses you, but love your enemy.
- Realize that the glory belongs to the Lord and is not a thing to be coveted or heralded.
- Remember that today's trophy cup can quickly become tomorrow's cup of sorrow, but obedience to God will eventually be rewarded.
- Align with noble, trustworthy friends who show no signs of jealousy and who will lovingly tell you the truth at all costs.
- Give yourself permission to make mistakes and even grieve over them, but set a time limit on grieving.
- Don't step outside the boundaries God has set for you.
- Make sure you are where God calls you to be at all times by maintaining an attitude of prayer.
- If God calls you to the battlefield of crisis intercession, do not go looking for pleasure.

The prayer lines were always open between David and the Lord. When he was hated, God became his friend. When he lost his kingdom, God became his wealth. When he sinned, God became his refuge. When he failed, God became the lifter of his soul. When he lost his way, God became his guide. When he lost his strength, God became his shield. When he lost his dignity, God became his honor. Crisis intercessors are called to a oneness with God that is uninterupted by times of trouble. They need to see God in everything so they don't miss Him in anything.

The process of developing that kind of intimacy will most assuredly involve mistakes and misunderstandings, but David's life gives testimony to God's unfathomable ability to turn our failures into stepping-stones for greatness.

You may have launched out as a crisis intercessor and met with a Saul who has you on the run. Perhaps you have encountered a crisis and failed to intercede. If so, read the psalms and learn to pray them. Know that God will do for you what He did for David. Ask the Lord to turn your times of running back into times of reigning.

Pick up your slingshot of prayer and conquer the crisis for heaven's sake!

PERSONAL REFLECTION

Are You a Crisis Intercessor?

1. Are you commonly awakened with an urgent need to pray about a person, place or problem?
2. In your regular times of prayer, are you often struck with the sense of a pending emergency?
3. Do you thrive in times of crisis?

4. Is your daily routine often interrupted with a call to pray about a face, a name or a situation you have witnessed?

5. Do you find you have no rest in prayer until the crisis is over or until you have the assurance that your assignment is completed?

Notes

1. Beth Alves, *Becoming a Prayer Warrior* (Ventura, CA: Regal Books, 1998), pp. 29, 30.

2. A. Canfield, *A Cup of Chicken Soup for the Soul*, pp. 186, 187, quoted in Dutch Sheets, *The River of God* (Ventura, CA: Regal Books, 1998), pp. 214, 215.

CHAPTER 8

WARFARE INTERCESSORS

PARTNERS WITH TRUTH

All spiritual warfare is a fight over one thing: TRUTH. Jesus said: "I am the way, and the *truth*, and the life; no one comes to the Father, but through Me" (John 14:6, italics added)—meaning that Satan's aggressions against us will always be waged over our ability to grasp and appropriate the truth found in Him. He also said, "Apart from Me you can do nothing" (John 15:5)—meaning that we know truth and flourish in it only to the degree that we stay dependent upon Jesus the Word, or Truth, made flesh (see John 1:14). The belief that *living independently of God is good* is the ultimate lie from Satan. The Bible warns that the devil will come to steal truth from us (see Matt. 13:19). But if he cannot steal it, he will try to plant lies within the truth we already know (see Matt. 13:25). It's time to blow the whistle on this vile deceiver and unmask some of his devious tactics!

FEARFULLY MADE

You and I were created with the ability to fear. The Bible defines fear two ways: Fear can mean reverence or awe; it can also mean terror or fright. Awe or reverence releases us to enter God's rest and receive His power, while terror or fright paralyzes the heart's ability to communicate with the head and destroys its ability to function. And so, to be released into our anointed place in prayer, we begin by fearing God in truth—giving Him awe, gratitude and reverence (see Isa. 30:15; Ps. 100; John 1). The more we hear and declare His truth, the more His life is able to pump forth out of the chambers of our hearts and be released into our minds so "that [we] may prove what the will of God is, that which is good and acceptable and perfect" (Rom. 12:2).

And what is His good, acceptable and perfect will? That we become heirs! The promises in the Bible are our inheritance. Therefore, as we discover God's "awe"-some promises and begin to lay claim to them, the devil will attempt to deceive us with awful counterfeits or lies. His greatest strategy is to provoke us into an unholy fear, or intimidation, of authority figures. Then, as we are terrorized by authority, we will transfer that fear to the works God has set apart for us to do and be afraid to trust the Lord as the supreme authority in our lives.

ACCUSATION, SATAN'S WAY TO DIVIDE AND CONQUER

The enemy uses relentless accusation to keep us from accepting God as a protective authority. The Bible refers to Satan as "the accuser of our brethren" (Rev. 12:10). He tries to convince us that it is God who is accusing us. Then, if we do not know the truth about God as a loving authority, we will not only agree with the accuser's lies but also become like him and begin to accuse ourselves and others. Accusation spawns a fear of being known and breeds disunity. Finally, as a divided Body, we are rendered powerless and ultimately become a destructive force for the enemy in preventing God's will from being done upon the earth.

Warfare intercessors are the ones who fight to usher in truth by establishing God's authority in places where Satan has a stronghold on people, problems and places. They are the military might of prayer. Some warfare intercessors have been anointed with spiritual perception to discern the evil spirits that reign over various territories; others have been anointed with strategies for establishing God's authority in places where the devil has taken both spiritual and physical ground. George Otis, Jr., is a research intercessor who has been anointed to do both.

Declaring the Truth in the Face of Fear

I (Tommi) can think of few people who have done as much to inform God's warriors about the enemy's lies as George Otis, Jr. He is a brilliant research intercessor who has provided the Church with incredibly valuable information for spiritual warfare. I have a hallowed regard for this man as one who has been entrusted with enormous authority for God. I tell you this about him so you will understand how the deceiver, Satan, can use our fear (intimidation) of authority to prevent us from obeying the Lord.

I was at the Spiritual Warfare Network conference in Southern California when Lisa Otis, George's wife, entered the prayer room to share that she was pregnant. The results from her blood tests had just come in and her obstetrician suspected that their baby might be Down's syndrome, a "water baby." We prayed for healing and a safe delivery. Jenna was born perfect!

Then, years later, on a visit to George's parents in Simi Valley, California, Jenna managed to slip outside without notice. At the Holy Spirit's nudging, George's mother scanned the backyard and spied her granddaughter's fully-clad body lying motionless near the deep end of the swimming pool. An unforgettable drama began to unfold. They rushed Jenna to the hospital and called for prayer—not knowing how long she had been in the water. Jenna lay in a coma, suspended between life and death.

I received the call to join their global prayer alert on my way out the door to speak at an Aglow meeting that evening. Thousands had been summoned into intercession worldwide through the 700 Club, the Voice of Hope radio network and even the Internet. While driving and praying, I could not ignore a riveting compulsion to turn on Christian radio. The pastor was teaching on 1 Peter 5:8: "Your adversary, the devil, prowls about like a roaring lion, seeking someone to devour." He explained that the word "devour" can mean to swallow up or to drown.

As soon as possible, I looked up the word in *Strong's Concordance* to confirm its meaning. Assured that the meaning was correct, I then began to pray against the spirit of the devourer that had called the Otis's daughter to the water, even from the time she was in the womb, in order to drown her. I reasoned that the Otises knew LOTS about spiritual warfare, so I wavered about sending them this information. The accuser began to taunt me with thoughts such as, *Who do you think you are? You are insignificant compared to the spiritual giants that surround this family.* Finally, I wrote a brief note anyway.

My input was alluded to in George's follow-up article entitled "Out of the Depths: A Tale of Death Denied":

Caught inside our own slow-motion universe, Lisa and I became increasingly aware that a fierce spiritual battle was being waged over Jenna. Having stalked our daughter from conception, the Adversary was closing in to "devour" his sweet meat—an action which, in the Greek, literally means "to swallow up" or "to drown."[1]

Jenna is perfect—no complications from the near-drowning incident and no further problems. I had pushed through my fear to approach authority with a timely piece of the puzzle, and God had used that knowledge to expose a truth to one of His generals!

CHOOSE THIS DAY WHOM YOU WILL SERVE

Generals are those who govern in positions of authority because they have obeyed while walking under authority. Their authority is delegated to them by God and is maintained through obedience to God, or to the Word, which is God's ultimate authority. Obedience to God's Word is the mortar of our might in spiritual warfare (see Josh. 1:8). If we do not know God's Word, our ignorance can destroy us (see Hos. 4:6).

Sin, unforgiveness and rebellion render us impotent and prove that we are living independently of God (see 1 Sam. 15:23; Isa. 59:2). Sin causes people to come under Satan's authority and binds them from being free to obey God (see Rom. 8:7). Therefore, warfare intercessors are those who fight to reestablish God's authority in places where people have lost their freedom to choose dependence upon Him. A victim is merely a person without a choice. A victor is a person who has exercised his or her choice and won! The joy of warfare intercession lies in opening the door of choice to victims.

A victim is merely a person without a choice. A victor is a person who has exercised his or her choice and won!

You and I have been granted authority by God to protect and provide for people, not to control or confuse them with manipulation. We have been empowered to prevent evil from killing, robbing and destroying heaven's purposes and plans for people upon the earth. Isaiah 58:6,7 defines our mission:

- To bring deliverance to people in bondage so they can be set free from every kind of oppression
- To provide for the needy
- To cover those who are naked (or being exploited through lack)
- To make ourselves accessible to relatives who need our help

Our mission could not be more clear.

PARTNER WITH TRUTH, NOT PLEASURE

Many in the Church, however, are still living for "[their] own pleasure" (Isa. 58:13) rather than entering the fight to establish God's truth in places where exploitation has submerged people in cesspools of debilitating hopelessness. We are often more worried about doing our thing than we are about doing God's thing. Some even ask, "If God is so powerful, why does He need my prayers at all?" Dutch Sheets brilliantly answers that question in his best-seller *Intercessory Prayer:*

> So complete and final was Adam's authority over the earth that he, not just God, had the ability to give it to another! . . . Adam handed it to Satan, Satan offered it to Jesus if Jesus would worship him. . . . So complete and final was God's decision to do things on earth through human beings that it cost God the Incarnation to regain what Adam gave away. He had to become a part of the human race. . . . Without question, *humans were forever to be God's link to authority and activity on the earth.* . . . God chose, from the time of Creation, to work on earth *through* people, not independent of them. He has and always will, even at the cost of becoming one. Though God is sovereign and all-powerful, Scripture tells us that He limited Himself, concerning the affairs of earth, to working through human beings.[2]

As humans with a choice to become a link between either the kingdom of light or the kingdom of darkness, every decision we make, every word we speak, every action we take either links us to God's authority or to Satan's.

WRESTLE FOR THOSE WHO DON'T RECOGNIZE THE FIGHT

Ephesians 6:12 says that we "do not wrestle against flesh and blood, but against principalities, against powers, against the rulers of the darkness of this age, against spiritual hosts of wickedness in the heavenly places" *(NKJV)*. Our fight is spiritual; therefore, most of the world doesn't even recognize it.

Do you remember the movie classic *The Wizard of Oz,* which hyped the works of darkness? Dorothy and her three misguided friends followed the yellow brick road looking for a power that eventually proved to be a charade. It took Toto, Dorothy's terrier, to pull back the curtain and expose the counterfeit of a false image projected on a screen. Someone once said, "It's not the size of the dog in the fight, it's the size of the fight in the dog that determines the outcome!" Warfare intercessors are called to fight like a dog to draw back the drapes that camouflage darkness. They are the ones who prayerfully battle to unveil the lies and false images that have been projected upon the mental screens in deceived minds.

Because Satan is a spirit being, when he taps on people's shoulders or whispers in their ears, they think the culprit is you or me or someone made of flesh and blood. Our enemy instigates his vulturous plans with abhorrent anonymity.

Exposing the Lie When You've Caused the Hurt

If Satan can convince parents, teachers and other authority figures to somehow wound a child and then convince that child to respond with an inner vow to never be hurt by authority again, he can manipulate that child like a puppet. That's exactly what happened to Sven Sjarlsberg. Sven's biological father died when he was 12, and his mother remarried a monstrously cruel alcoholic man two years later. His stepfather mocked him, beat him and tried to control his every move. Ingrid, Sven's mom, was passive and, though she loved her son, felt helpless to intervene. By the time Sven was 16, he was a runaway on the streets, begging for money to buy alcohol and drugs.

In the meantime, Ingrid had met Jesus. Initially, her conversion caused her husband, Carl, to became even more rigid, so she found support in a prayer group of women who were all focused on interceding for their husbands and children. Many of these women were savvy in spiritual warfare, and their prayers, combined with biblical strategies, eventually brought results.

Ingrid started to serve Carl as though he were a godly man, without ever saying a word about Christ. The years passed and Carl finally began to soften. Then one morning he asked Ingrid if he could accompany her to church. Her spirit rejoiced—though wisdom told her not to show it. That morning Carl gave his heart to Jesus and was instantly delivered from alcoholism. He also felt an overwhelming sense of remorse for the way he had treated Sven. Together Carl and Ingrid began to employ the warfare tactics learned at the prayer meetings.

They prayed the Scriptures daily over Sven's life. Both Ingrid and Carl wept before Sven, taking responsibility for the incredible pain they had caused him. Sven did not forgive them. He hated his mother for not protecting him; he hated Carl for the hurts he could not forgive. Sven hated all authority, especially God's. He mocked the Church and called Christians weaklings who needed a crutch. Satan had blinded him to the fact that his alcohol and drugs were an even greater crutch. Sven became a womanizer with a deep need to hurt women. He was in and out of jail for his violent outbursts, but his parents refused to give up hope.

Year after year, they visited Sven regularly but never said a word about Jesus; they simply modeled God's love. Each time they went to Sven's apartment, they also brought along something to penetrate Satan's spiritual hold on Sven's life. Ingrid had copied pages and pages of Scripture and then burned the pages until they turned to ash. She poured the ashes all around the outside of Sven's apartment, asking God to bring beauty out of the ashes (see Isa. 61:3). She also asked the women in her group to anoint a prayer cloth that she cut into tiny pieces and planted around Sven's apartment. Carl carried a small vial of oil and would anoint his hands before embracing Sven; he did this to call forth God's power upon Sven's life. One time Ingrid found Sven's shoes in the bathroom and pulled up the lining where she wrote Scriptures; she was performing a symbolic act to represent the fact that he would one day walk in the Word of God.

Ten long years passed and nothing seemed to work. Then one day, Carl noticed a lump on his neck; it was only one of many tumors that had subtly metastasized throughout his body. His earthly life was about to end, but his victory in death was just beginning. When Sven heard the news of his stepfather's terminal condition, he rushed to his bedside. For three months Carl mentored the boy—now a man—whom he had so deeply wounded years before. They cried together and forgave each other for years and years of hurt.

Sven also realized how he had judged his mother and, because of that judgment, was unable to have a healthy relationship with any woman. He asked God to forgive him for judging both of his parents and believing the lie that God was responsible for his pain. He took all of his hurts to the Cross and nailed them there. Then, just before he died, Carl witnessed the restorative power of God when he had the privilege of leading Sven, his stepson, to Christ.

The warfare had not been easy, nor had it been immediate—but it was eternal! Today, Sven is in the ministry, working with youth in Sweden. He offers a message of truth to those who are addicted to drugs and alcohol because of their rejection and deep-rooted judgments toward authority. He's bent on exposing the lies that almost cost him his life!

Fit for the Fight

Those who have eyes to discern the enemy and tenaciously fight on the front lines can only do so when they are physically, spiritually and emotionally fit. Weak and weary soldiers drain and dilute the troops. I (Tommi) learned this lesson firsthand on a prayer journey to Cambodia.

We arrived in Phnom Penh in October 1995. This abscessed city had been dedicated to the spirit of death, and we knew that much intercession would be needed to stand against its venomous sting. Prior to our departure from the United States, a nurse on our team wrenched her back, requiring chiropractic care and heavy doses of pain medication. I suggested she cancel her plane reservations, but she desperately wanted to be included. Prayer journeys and prayer teams were new then and we had not yet established our current policies. We now realize that spiritual warfare is too intense to engage in with wounded warriors shuffling through the ranks.

Permit me to explain. The flight to Cambodia only stiffened her already inflamed back. I felt angry at Satan for using this well-intentioned intercessor to become a diversion to our strategy. When we landed, she asked for a wheelchair, but I insisted she walk off the plane: "You will put your foot on the land! If God has called you to this land, you must step on it. His Word says, 'Every place on which the sole of your foot treads, I have given it to you'" (Josh. 1:3). She walked off the plane and that was it! This dear woman of God lay flat on her back for the majority of our prayer journey.

Though she spent much of the trip praying for us, our focus on spiritual combat was diverted. She could not dress, bathe or attend to any of her private needs alone. Our living conditions were very primitive, making matters even more difficult for all involved. Because the potholes in the roads were two and three feet deep, the drive to the Killing Fields was torturous for her. Every bounce stimulated a greater spasm in her back. Knowing that Satan generally attacks through the weakest link, we could not leave this dear one uncovered. Daily, we were compelled to leave a team member behind to pray with and guard over her.

Even leaving the country became a pressure-packed ordeal. Wondering how we would transport her to the airport, our wearied team interceded and the Lord raised up a French doctor who graciously injected her with a spinal block. She finally walked! We later realized that a person who begins a prayer journey in a weakened condition will become tempting prey for the ruling spirits over that land. Without prayer coverage, she might have lost her life. Though God covered us, and our mission was accomplished, we all knew that her presence had strained the team.

BECOMING WELL "SOULED"

Not only must a warfare intercessor be physically fit for the fight, but his or her soul must also be healthy. Unforgiveness is a cancer on the soul. Its decaying effect can rust our prayer shields and rot our spiritual fruitfulness. Unforgiveness breeds suspicion, gossip, ingratitude and a host of other maladies in our lives. It opens the floodgate to the enemy's control. We cannot fight effectively against the author of hatred while strains of bitterness weave their vile threads through our minds, wills and emotions.

Preparation for doing battle on the front lines includes taking an internal inventory and examining our hearts before the Lord (see Ps. 51). The heritage of the believer encompasses the freedom to overlook offenses. On the other hand, if we have offended others, we can and should make every effort to accept responsibility and provide restitution. In either case, we dare not forget that only the one who has been offended has the power to dispense the healing balm of forgiveness. Has someone hurt you? Have you hurt others? Take it to the Cross and nail it there. We cannot effectively battle against the strongholds in the lives of others until we have dealt with our own.

The Word, Our Spiritual Fitness Center

With the Cross as our legacy and our mission before us, victory will rest upon our spiritual fitness. It's not the boulders that topple giants, it's the pebbles. We must pay attention to the basics—the daily "little" habits that strengthen our grip and empower our walk: prayer, praise and proclaiming the Word. God's Word embodies all that He is. Therefore, if you want to know what you are to be, do or say, you will find your "marching orders" in the Bible.

Clearly, every Christian should learn to "put on the whole armor of God" (see Eph. 6, *NKJV*), apply the blood, secure his or her authority in Jesus' name and maintain an attitude of repentance, but those who are engaging the enemy in intercessory warfare need to keep their swords unsheathed at all times. Begin to pray the Word and root it in your spirit. Meditate upon it. Memorize it. Believe that it has the power to do all that God promises.

Be Prepared . . . You're Never a Tourist!

On a trip to India, I (Tommi) learned that spiritual warfare intercessors are never casual bystanders or observers; we are never tourists. We are always on duty, even when we're on vacation. Wherever we are, we have been strategically placed there by God and need to be prepared for battle.

After a long flight and an overnight train ride, our 32 hours of sleepless travel left us feeling exhausted—no way to start a prayer journey! We were excited to explore the terrain. Now traveling by jeep, we had a clear view of every Durga temple and began drinking in the sights as though we were there as tourists. India was celebrating Durga, an erotic and demonic goddess festival—nothing short of nasty!

Suddenly, I became so sick in my stomach that I begged, "Please stop the jeep!" My body was overcome with nausea and I left a gross pile of all but my guts on the roadside. We traveled a little further up the road when the same thing happened again and again. I had never been that sick to my stomach before.

I could feel a blanket of incredible evil wrapping itself around me. We stopped at the base of a statue where once again I experienced a complete lack of control over my intestines. A group of men surrounded our jeep, demanding money for the festival; but Bindu Choudhrie, one of the women on the team, confronted them, saying, "We don't worship your god, so why should we give to you?" She pointed to an emblem of the Cross on our windshield. They left.

Our driver finally pulled into a rest area that offered a dirty cot and primitive toilet facilities. We could only imagine how many people had stretched out there before me, but I was too overcome to care. I turned to Marilyn Luschen and Bindu and said, "Ladies, you've got to do spiritual warfare over me!" Their naive response only added to my pain: "How?"

There I was, doubled over, holding my head and trying to train the troops in the midst of battle: "Pray, pray, pray . . . sing songs about the blood of Jesus. Call upon His name." Two hours later I was healed.

I finally climbed back into the jeep and asked, "Lord, what happened back there? What was the open door?"

The imprint of His answer is forever stamped upon my mind: "You're never a tourist in the land! You arrived on one of the most demonic worship days of the Hindu calendar and didn't cover yourself or pray as you passed the temples. Every time you went by a place of sacrifice, they were offering up new prayers, new incantations."

Today we insist that every person be trained in spiritual warfare before invading the enemy's territory!

COMBAT IN KOREA

In 1993, Beth and I (Tommi) attended a Gideon's Army Conference at the Methodist prayer mountain on the outskirts of Seoul, Korea. There, a gifted prophet anointed Beth's pointer finger and confidently declared that it would be like the finger of God. We left the conference excited about the Lord's plans for the prayer journey that was to follow.

I had agreed to be part of the first Praying Through the 10/40 Window project, which targets the countries that lie between the latitudes of 10 and 40 and are often referred to as the least evangelized areas in the world. Therefore, having invested several months in training the team for spiritual battle, I intended to lead it throughout North Korea as Tommi Femrite, member of New Life Church—not as an executive with Intercessors International.

Less than a month before we were to leave, Beth decided that Intercessors International needed to be involved. In my thinking, I was still the leader. I had formed the team; I had filled out all the applications; I had registered as the leader. Now, suddenly, Beth was coming.

Assured that God had called me to lead this small army into warfare, I gathered everyone together for a briefing. Those who were not from my city were joining us for the first time, including Beth. Suddenly I noticed that Beth kept taking the leadership away from me. I could sense a power struggle gripping our wills. The spirits of disunity and division over the land were beginning to manifest in our midst. If I said up, Beth said down. We both knew something wasn't right. We called a time out and went to another room. Our conversation went something like this:

"Beth, what is going on?"

"Well, I'm trying to lead the team, Tommi."

"Beth, why are you trying to lead the team? I am the leader."

"No, you're not. I am the president of the ministry—the team leader."

"But Beth, God called me to lead this team."

"Listen, Tommi, God called me to lead this team as Moses."

"Well, Beth, God called me to lead this team as Jo-shu-a!"

Suddenly we understood what was happening. We were both to be team leaders. Beth was to stay back and intercede with three intercessors while I spied out the land with four others. She maintained the home base; I stepped onto the battlefield. Because we have a habit of keeping short accounts and not letting the enemy get a foothold, we were able to maintain a united team.

We really work at staying emotionally current. If we had not already cultivated that practice at home, we would have stepped right into the web of division our enemy had so subtly set before us.

The following day, I left with my research team for the DMZ (de-militarized zone) on the border between North and South Korea. It's an eerie place, hosting a looming tower and a building that vividly sum up the spirit of division entrenched in the land. A long trail of tape stretches down the side of the building's interior and across the floor, up over the table and back again, dividing North and South Korea in half. Microphones are stationed at the exact center of the table. Because we were foreigners, the only place in North Korea we were allowed to enter was on the north side of this room. We swiftly spied out the situation and went home to set up a mock village in order to form a prayer strategy.

While we were spying out the land, Beth's team used a map of the DMZ to pray for us. They laid books at the various places on the map to simulate buildings and kept a prayer journal, recording the words the Lord gave them in intercession. We later discovered that the times and places where we were in the most danger paralleled their strongest intercession.

Three days later, we returned with a full team as guests for a VIP tour arranged by the general of the South Korean Army—a Christian who had attended the Gideon's Army Conference. We had been warned not to point because an outstretched hand could be mistaken for a gun. But with Beth's anointed finger, a spiritual weapon was about to be unleashed! Our first stop was the lookout tower. Beth inconspicuously directed her anointed pointer by rubbing her nose, scratching her arm and saying, "The enemy will not cross this line!" We later learned that 300,000 North Korean troops had marched to the border but did not cross. The press reported that it was as if an invisible line had been drawn—and we know the One who drew it!

Next, we ambled over to the DMZ building, completing our prophetic acts along the way. Each member of our team carried two sticks. We had written North Korea on one stick and South Korea on the other. Based on the example set forth in Ezekiel 37:15-28, we held the sticks in our hands as if they were one stick, declaring that Korea would be one nation serving only one God and one king, Jesus. Finally, inside the building, we whispered hushed prayers: "See that guard over there, he's going to know Jesus as his Lord and Savior." Just three days prior, the guards were scowling; this day, they were actually grinning. Amazingly, North Korean guards were even volunteering to have their pictures taken with us.

Though they all bore M-16 rifles, our fears were silenced as our faith surged into the heavenlies: "You're going to come to Jesus!" One of our strategies had been to plant the Word of God in the land. We wrote Scriptures on twigs and dropped them randomly on the ground. Thankfully, no one noticed, because our lives could have been in jeopardy.

It was as though the Lord had blinded the eyes of the enemy. Some of the local Korean intercessors who had joined our team were refugees from North Korea and didn't have security clearances; therefore, they never expected to go to the border house. We knew that God had cleared the way so we could enter the land with both North and South Koreans praying as one. It was a miracle! God had given the plan and we had carried out the work.

Research Intercessors

If God has anointed you for warfare intercession, know all you can about the person, people group, policy or place that is the target of your intercession. I (Beth) have recruited five research intercessors who meticulously compile and document details about the spiritual ground being covered in prayer. Research intercessors thrive on prayerfully collecting vital facts about strongholds and principalities. They help us to formulate our plan of attack.

Intercessors on the front lines are incredibly enriched by the input of research intercessors.

Intercessors on the front lines are incredibly enriched by the input of research intercessors. The more data we have, the more precisely we can streamline our strategy. Though most intercessors can discern the fruits of the adversary's efforts, an informed intercessor understands the root system and has the ability to annihilate that root system with precision prayer.

When Jesus passed the fig tree, He cursed the root of it (see Matt. 21:19-21). That tree's former shell remained, but its power to reproduce was forever arrested. We, too, must speak to the spiritual roots that have anchored people in deception. But first we have to identify them—and we can't do it alone.

HOME-BASED INTERCESSORS

You don't have to go to another nation to do spiritual warfare. It can be done over your own home, neighborhood, city or nation. Just remember: Even the Lone Ranger needed a Tonto to help him scout out the land and to support him when the going got tough. Warfare is exhausting, so be sure you have an Aaron and a Hur (see Exod. 17) to back you up. We cannot contest the forces of darkness alone and expect to win. When Tommi or I (Beth) enter a foreign land, we sometimes ask hundreds of people to pray for us.

Entering unfamiliar territory means confronting unchallenged powers and principalities, rulers of darkness that have set up fierce and stringent root systems. Because we have encountered the adversary's backlash on the mission field, we realize the importance of home-based intercessors—and so does the Lord! Those who shield others in prayer at home share the spiritual reward with the ones on the front lines. We depend upon our spiritual covering to succeed, and so must you! Remember: Loners are usually losers—so stay connected with like-minded warriors!

PITFALLS OF WARFARE INTERCESSORS

Believing that we can win the battle alone is but one of the many pitfalls that seem to entrap the warfare intercessor. Others include:

- Forgetting to deal with issues of unresolved personal conflict before entering the battle
- Viewing every prayer need as a battle and thereby neglecting intimacy with the Lord
- Entering the battle with a personal agenda rather than with the team's agenda
- Refusing to submit to the one in authority
- Going to war without counting the cost
- Having no battle plan
- Allowing distractions to sidetrack the mission
- Rushing ahead of the Lord's timing
- Marching out without intercessory covering
- Running from battle to battle without taking time to rest and refuel
- Becoming overly aggressive and not making room for others' giftings
- Being naive about strategies for warring against the backlash
- Neglecting to prepare for retaliation after victory by prayerfully maintaining the spiritual ground

JEHOSHAPHAT—MAN OF WAR, MAN OF PEACE

By probing the biography of valorous King Jehoshaphat in 2 Chronicles 20, we discover God's prototype for the triumphant warfare intercessor. His strategy in dealing with the enemy ensured an uninterrupted victory. When Jehoshaphat received news that the mighty "ites"—the Moabites, Ammonites and Meunites—were pursuing him to make war, he bowed in complete attentiveness to the Lord.

After an in-depth read through his story, we have extracted many lessons. We hope that you will take the time to read the story for yourself and allow the Lord to show you even more insights. The following are some of the principles of war and peace we have uncovered from Jehoshaphat's legacy:

- Call other warriors together for prayer and fasting.
- Become accountable to God and other trusted intercessors.
- Establish trust in the Lord by declaring, "Thou wilt hear and deliver us" (v. 9).
- Pursue holiness and maintain intimacy with the Lord.
- Know the names of your enemies and recruit the aid of research intercessors for information about their strategies.
- Keep your focus on the Lord and don't try to win in your own strength.
- Allow His Word to become your fortress.
- Maintain open lines of communication with those who are standing with you so unity will prevail.
- "Put your trust in His prophets and succeed" (v. 20).
- When God gives you the battle plan, obey it.
- Stand firm and refuse discouragement.
- Worship the Lord with praise, thanksgiving and song.
- Forge ahead with faith and stay away from negative people.
- Expect to leave the battle enriched with plunder.
- Rejoice in the Lord for the victory.
- Know that the enemy will attempt to retaliate through a false sense of peace toward the future.
- Do not build bridges with the enemy.
- Beware of establishing unholy alliances with those who do not share your focus in faith.

Jehoshaphat's ability to stand strong in warfare and trust God with such resoluteness might leave us wondering how he could possibly have later opened the door to wickedness. The lesson here is that times of victory are not meant to turn us into celebrities; they should instead stretch us so that we are even more prepared for the future. We must persevere—too many souls are at stake. Although there will be casualties and calamities, the rewards will one day outweigh the pain—and our retirement benefits will be eternal! We can't do everything, but we can do something.

Praise the Lord and pass the ammunition!

—————— **PERSONAL REFLECTION** ——————
Are You a Warfare Intercessor?

1. Are you angered by injustices?
2. When you see others in pain, do you instantly want to wrestle with the enemy for their freedom?
3. Do you thrive on compiling research about spiritual roots and governing principalities?
4. Are you apt to move out in forcefulness in your prayer time?
5. Do you look for the battle when you are praying?
6. Do you struggle with sitting still at prayer meetings where the enemy is not being confronted?

Notes
1. This article was included in a newsletter to the intercessors from Global Harvest Ministries, August 23, 1995.
2. Dutch Sheets, *Intercessory Prayer* (Ventura, CA: Regal Books, 1996), pp. 28, 29.

CHAPTER 9

WORSHIP INTERCESSORS

∞

$\mathscr{S}$ACRED ROMANCERS

It is possible to worship God without loving Him, but it is impossible to love God without worshiping Him. Worship is the lifeblood of our relationship with the Trinity. It is the antidote to the blahs and rouses the ho-hum pray-er into passionate intimacy with the Lord. Worship is to the soul what water is to the body. Therefore, no Christian can drink only once in a while without becoming parched and weary.

Heaven's water fountain flows for all who will come and fill their empty cups with worship. The water of worship is the soul's cleansing agent, providing an internal bath for soiled hearts and minds. Soaking at the well of worship is the way to enter God's presence and receive His rest. It is the way to quiet the human mind so the Lord can speak His purposes and plans into our lives. Worship sets the ambiance for times of sacred romance between God and those who love Him. Every human heart is custom crafted with a need for worship.

The Refuge of Worship

Worship was an essential part of Jesus' upbringing. Let's not forget that He was born to Jewish parents and raised in a Jewish home. Undoubtedly, Jesus wore a tallith, or prayer shawl, when He prayed. The word "tallith" means cloak. It is used even today by Orthodox and Conservative Jews for a head covering as they daily worship God. Dedicated Jews commonly cover their entire heads with the tallith to keep themselves from being distracted by the outside world.

Because I (Karen) am married to Dennis, a Christian with very religious Jewish roots, I have become a curious student of the worship that surrounds his spiritual legacy. Recently, an Orthodox Jewish business associate of his told me that he uses the tallith as a "refuge" while repeating the Shema—the traditional two-page prayer that is read each morning and evening in Jewish homes. The Shema begins: "Hear O Israel, the Lord, our God, the Lord is One. Blessed be the name of His glorious majesty forever and ever. Thou shalt love the Lord thy God with all thy heart, with all thy soul, and with all thy might." Not only is the reading of the Shema carefully observed in Orthodox homes, but the psalms are also memorized from childhood and prayed at least three times a day as an adult.

Religious Jews even wear straps that wrap around the fingers and wind up the arms, over the head and around the heart, symbolizing the fact that they are bound to the Torah (the first five books in the Old Testament). These straps are a reminder that the Word is to travel from the hand to the head to the heart. Throughout the day, an Orthodox Jew will often be seen softly drumming his chest in a "daven," or prayer, as he pounds the psalms into his heart. Conservative and Orthodox Jews begin their Sabbath shortly after dusk because the night preceded daylight during Creation. Nearly everything about Jewish tradition is somehow related to the worship of God and His Word.

The Jews' rich heritage of worship has taught them the value of celebration. Until you have been to a Jewish wedding, you don't really know what it means to party. Until you have celebrated at a Jewish table, you don't fully understand the meaning of a feast. It's no wonder that God has based the celebration of His Son's return around this awesome group of worshipers!

A Circumcised Heart

The old covenant, or contract, between Abraham—the father of the Jews—and God was sealed through circumcision (see Gen. 17:11), cutting off the flesh on the most private part of a man. The circumcision ceremony, which is today called the Brith Milah, ends with the prayer, "May the boy grow in vigor of mind and body to a love of the Torah, to the marriage canopy, and to a life of good deeds." This tradition so angered Zipporah, the Midianite wife of Moses, that she called him "a bridegroom of blood" (Exod. 4:26).

Today, we Christians are under a new covenant. We have failed at living "a life of good deeds" according to the laws of the Torah (see Rom. 2:25). Therefore, Jesus became our "Bridegroom of blood." He cut Himself off from the Father and shed His own blood to remit our sins. He then left us a sword (the Bible) to use in circumcising the "flesh" or sinful human attributes tucked deep within the most private part of our hearts.

Under the new covenant, we are not bound by talliths, the ritualistic reading of the Shema, or straps that wrap around our flesh; we are bound by cords of love that are woven by faith around His redemptive cross and His life-changing Word. The truth of what

He has done for us is our cause for worship—it is the power of our warfare, the fuel of our mercy, the reason we rejoice in all things.

WHEN WORSHIP LOSES ITS JOY

Worship creates an attitude of gratitude—softening calloused hearts, healing desolate lands and rectifying impossible situations. From Genesis to Revelation, worship is the key to ushering in God's presence. Without worship, the world is a sad place. Though the Jews typically used tambourines, cymbals, trumpets, flutes and lyres to strengthen their worship, just prior to the Middle Ages this custom was replaced with a stifling restraint of all musical instrumentation in Jewish synagogues. The twentieth century has brought a slight reform, but this lack is still a loss worth mourning.

Today, all that remains of Solomon's Temple in Israel is the Wailing Wall. A place once noted for its celebration of God with expressive instruments, joyful singing and animated dancing has now become a place of solemnity. This sad commentary is indicative of all worship that loses its freedom as people impose their control over what the Lord called good. God has a plan for worship and that plan is orderly, but it is also liberating. It must be carried out God's way if it is going to bring in His presence and our abandon to His will.

A SACRED SIGHT FOR SURRENDERED EYES

The worship offered by Cain and Abel (see Gen. 4) exemplifies two heart attitudes: one honors God, the other honors man. Abel offered a lamb—a symbol of dependence upon the Good Shepherd. But Cain offered the fruit of the earth—his own works. Worship that is offered in spirit and in truth is a statement of dependence; it is our ultimate act of surrender.

In Psalm 51:17, the Lord shares the key to godly worship. Let's read it together:

> The sacrifices of God are a broken spirit; a broken and a contrite heart.

Just as the earth must be broken in order to bring forth fruit, the self-protection around our hearts must be penetrated to fully experience God in worship.

Whether our worship is public or private, the issue is always the condition of our hearts.

I (Karen) will never forget the embarrassment I felt about worship when I first became a believer. I began my walk with the Lord in the early '70s at the Basic Youth Conflicts seminar and later attended Pastor Jack Hayford's church. Pushing through my pride to lift my hands in public worship was a real struggle. Later, however, the Lord broke me even further when I was called out at a women's Aglow meeting to dance before the group. Insisting that dancing was foreign to my phlegmatic

Scandinavian background, I breathed an SOS prayer, asking God to strike me with a bolt of lightning—anything seemed better than surrendering to that kind of red-faced humiliation! Before long, the group was singing and I was dancing ever so awkwardly before them.

Obviously, I didn't die, but something broke in me that released a freedom to be real in the Lord's presence. Guardedness in worship can expose the fear of relinquishing control to the Lord in other areas of our lives as well.

Whether our worship is public or private, the issue is always the condition of our hearts. Raised hands that are sullied with sin and unforgiveness can either be lifted in pride before God or with the childlike hope that God will wash them, kiss them and blow away the dirt of the past. In Psalm 141:2, King David said, "May my prayer be counted as incense before Thee; the lifting up of my hands as the evening offering." When our hearts are right, our worship is an acceptable incense and offering before the Lord.

Entertaining Angels Unaware

Though we are *all* called to partake of worship's fruit, worship intercessors are those who are tuned in to heaven's audio chambers. When their hearts are rightly aligned, their spiritual antennas hear heaven's rhythm pumping out of the throne room on behalf of God's people. Worship may sound like the adulation of praise, the tearful song of mercy's identification, the victorious shouts and clapping of honor to the King of kings, the drumbeat of warfare or even a waltz of sacred romance.

Some worship intercessors will respond with musical instruments, others with songs (see Ps. 33:1-3). Some with dancing, others with clapping (see Ps. 150:4; 47:1). Some with bowing, others with raised hands (see Ps. 95:6; 141:2). The Lord determines the method; we simply obey. Worship intercession is used to either birth the release of our breakthroughs or to celebrate them after they have been fleshed out.

Even the most painful, dead places can be infused with life when a worship intercessor steps into the picture. Because mercy is one of my strongest gifts, I (Karen) often surprise my husband with long-term houseguests who have nowhere else to go. Diana was one of those people. I met her in a prayer circle at Church On The Way. A former missionary from New Zealand, she had run out of funds and become a disillusioned dropout on a traveling ministry team. What I didn't know about her is that she was an anointed worship intercessor.

Shortly after Diana arrived, I received a phone call that my son-in-law Andy's grandmother was critically ill. Grandma Frances was Jewish and, as far as I knew, had never heard the gospel. I grabbed my new roommate and dashed off to the convalescent home where Frances would spend her last couple of days on Earth. My heart swells with emotion when I recall that scene.

The spirit of despair drooped like a heavy tarp over the withered and feeble aged who lined the dimly lit hallways. We strolled into Grandma Frances's room where I tenderly shared about the awesome love of Jesus. Her condition was so frail that she was unable to verbally respond. When I finished praying, a peaceful glow shone upon her face; she squeezed my hand in response to heaven's invitation. What happened next took my breath away. Diana burst forth into a song that was so angelic even I felt as though I had touched heaven.

People in wheelchairs suddenly perked up and turned toward our room. The staff rushed down the hallway in disbelief. A woman lying in the bed across the room from Grandma Frances called out to me asking for prayer. The whole place was electrified. Worship had lifted the tarp of death and released the breath of eternal life.

A Time to Be Silent

Problems arise when those who are not anointed in worship intercession think that they are! I (Beth) am one of those who is NOT! Just to show you how bad it can get . . . when my daughter Julee was two years old, we were out running errands. As usual I was singing in the car, humming and making what I thought was a joyful noise unto the Lord. Suddenly, Julee flung both arms up to the sides of her head and plugged her innocent little fingers into her ears. "Mommy, please don't sing. Don't even go, 'hummm!'"

Realizing that this is not my area of anointing, I often recruit a worship intercessor to travel with me when I go out to minister. Joanna Virden is a former staff member at Intercessors International who has been a friend for years. Her prayers flow with singing that melts hardened hearts, heals broken bodies and sets captives free.

When Prayers Go Up in Smoke

Shortly after my childhood friend Pat Richardson came to know Christ, I invited her to join our Bible study. At that time, Pat was wrangling daily with an addiction to cigarettes. Every method she used to help her quit just spiraled her deeper into the addiction. The evening of our gathering, she had accidentally dropped her last fresh pack of cigarettes in the toilet. In desperation she dried them out in the toaster—this gal was really hooked!

Joanna Virden was at the gathering but had no idea about Pat's struggle. She simply began to pour out her heart in prayers that flowed into powerful songs of deliverance. As the singing continued, Pat said she heard the Lord thunder, "You need not ever smoke again!" The war with nicotine was finally over!

Worship's Residue

The power of worship intercession can linger for years. Carrie Hoffman's story proves my (Beth's) point. I had asked Carrie to join me on a speaking engagement in southern Germany back in the mid-'80s. While I dashed off to minister, she remained back in our hotel room to intercede for me. Closing her eyes to pray, the Lord shrouded Carrie's mind with the vision of a musical staff ribboning over the surrounding hills and valleys. Musical notes peppered the staff as it wound in and out of the houses that dotted the lush terrain. Before long, Carrie was caught up in a rhapsody of worship—clapping, singing and praying forth His Word.

In the meantime, a leader from the conference ran back upstairs to retrieve something from her room. She later said that when she opened the fire door to the hallway, an electrically charged wind blew against her face. People were gathered along the corridor in awe as they listened to Carrie worship.

As I said, that incident happened in the mid-'80s, and yet people are still testifying about it. Last year, while speaking in

the Alps, I asked a few people to stand up and share the circumstances leading to their conversion. A German woman explained
that late one night while lying in bed during the mid-'80s, songs
of worship that she had never heard before flowed over her as
though a musical staff was wrapping itself around her. When it
did, she surrendered her heart to Jesus. I could hardly wait to get
home to tell Carrie!

Pollinating the World with Hebraic Intercession

Another woman who accompanied me years ago was Bee
Whitley. Today Bee's focus is on illuminating the restoration of
our Jewish roots in worship by ushering in the power of God
through the use of dance, banners, paintings, elaborate sanctu-
ary drapings, altars and candles.

Back in the early '80s, Bee assembled a small dance team and
put together a collage of majestic banners. The dancers consisted of mothers and daughters, while fathers and sons carried the
banners. Hebraic worship of this kind was almost unheard of
back then, but she knew the call was definitely from the Lord.
When a neighboring church heard about the exciting results
that flowed from her worship team, they invited Bee and her
dancers to come. Bee still reflects on that time as one of the most
incredible events of her life. We'll let her talk:

When we arrived, our arms were loaded down with banners, and I could see that the music minister was feeling
a little intimidated. He sat resistantly behind a gorgeous
grand piano with a host of other musical instruments
gathered together as his backdrop. Then, as the proces-

sional of dancers wove graciously and artfully down the aisle, hoisting their royal banners, his face lit with God's glory. A spirit of worship descended upon the entire congregation. Suddenly, a thunderous roar—almost like the rush of many raging waters—clapped over that building. I have never heard anything like it before or since.

Today we are witnessing miraculous healings, both physical and spiritual, as the Lord is resurrecting the marriage between intercession and Hebraic worship.

On New Year's Eve in 1998, I was invited to minister during a 24-hour prayer vigil at a church in Washington, DC. About 2 A.M., I gathered the 30 people in attendance together to form a processional. We all grasped the edge of a long flowing red cloth and began our regal walk up the aisle. A female voice burst forth, "The church is one foundation!" The pastor pivoted to see who it was and began to weep. This dear woman had suffered a stroke and had been unable to speak, or walk without a cane, for a year. The flames of God's love danced upon our hearts as we celebrated her healing and His awesome power in worship intercession.

ASSEMBLY REQUIRED

Terry MacAlmon is the psalmist who gave birth to the popular song, "I Sing Praises." He is a gifted man who has served Intercessors International for many years. His anointing in worship intercession has changed an untold number of lives; he is a master of the grand piano. In 1992, Terry envisioned starting a worship center in Colorado Springs, where people from every denomination could gather together to worship the Lord. For a while, a small group gathered on Tuesday nights while the Lord led through Terry's anointing. Then one evening in the heart of worship, Terry slipped into an atypical state of travail. He felt as though he were standing all alone in the gap for worship. Intercession gave way to groaning. It also became the gateway to a dark time of burrowing into the wilderness.

God is faithful! He is the Resurrector
of Dead Dreams!

Season after disappointing season passed until he was finally dead to the vision he had once embraced so tightly. But God is faithful! He is the Resurrector of Dead Dreams! Today the Lord has rebirthed his vision through the World Prayer Center in Colorado Springs, Colorado. Terry has now launched a Wednesday noon worship session to restore Davidic worship unto the Lord. He fervently believes that one of the priorities the Church has lost is the marriage of worship and intercession. At the time of this writing, at least 40 churches and more than 400 people gather there weekly to participate and share in the vision. Worship changes things!

Worship Intercession, the Key to Breakthrough

Worship releases humanity's comfort and heaven's power. Whether you are feeling alienated or ambushed, worship intercession is the answer. It is the gag order we file against our enemy, the Christian's heavy-duty silencer against the terminator of hope. Worship is a safety net for those who are walking a tightrope of faith, an anesthesia for the heavyhearted. Worship is a bridge for those who long to come home, a wellspring for those who are thirsty along the way.

Worship intercessors are the ones who release the cannons of faith against walls of resistance. They carry spiritual artillery for breakthrough. Let's quickly browse through God's Word to gather just a few evidences of those who transformed situations by releasing the anointing of worship intercession:

- Abraham worshiped with his heart's treasure—his beloved son Isaac—and became the father of many nations (see Gen. 22).
- Moses worshiped with songs of remembrance after crossing the Red Sea and left a legacy for future generations (see Exod. 15:1-20).
- Joshua worshiped around the walls of Jericho with trumpet blasts and loud shouts and brought down the enemy's stronghold over a city (see Josh. 6:20).
- Hannah worshiped with petitions, vows and songs and watched the disgrace of personal barrenness transition into multiple births (see 1 Sam. 1—2).
- David worshiped with his harp and subdued the evil spirits that tormented his jealous rival, King Saul (see 1 Sam. 16:23).
- King David worshiped with dancing, at the expense of looking undignified before others, and won the approval of God (see 2 Sam. 6:16-21).
- Jehoshaphat worshiped with praise, thanksgiving and songs and brought forth victory in war (see 2 Chron. 20).

- Ezra and Nehemiah worshiped by calling for repentance, praise and Scripture reading and ushered in a great revival (see Neh. 8).
- Daniel worshiped with fasting while blessing the Lord and received supernatural revelation for interpreting the king's dream (see Dan. 1—2).
- Bartimaeus worshiped with words of faith and released his physical healing (see Mark 10:46-52).
- An unnamed woman worshiped with extravagant offerings that became the prophetic act pointing to Jesus' burial (see Mark 14:3,8).
- A prostitute worshiped with tears of gratitude at Jesus' feet and released the fragrance of God's mercy (see Luke 7:37-48).
- Stephen worshiped with cries of identificational repentance to release a spirit of conviction in Saul, who later became the apostle Paul (see Acts 6—7; 22:20).
- Paul and Silas worshiped while bound in a filthy dungeon and reaped a harvest of souls (see Acts 16:25-34).

In each of these situations, three common threads intertwine to form a sturdy cord for hauling in the breakthrough: sacrifice, sanctification and surrender. Worship intercession that ushers in God's presence must have all three—and cultivating those character traits always takes time. Remember: Spiritual growth is a process.

Sing Annie, Sing!

Annie Thompson is a seasoned worship intercessor who has spent much time in process. She has a gift not only for song but also for playing guitar. Months after my son-in-law was murdered, emotionally, I (Tommi), hit rock bottom. On one of those spiritually arid days, Annie called to say that she was driving more than an hour to come sing a song over me. I thought, *Why doesn't she just sing it over the phone?* But I was too weary to debate the issue. When she finally arrived, I understood. Her worship touched my heart so deeply that the carpet was saturated with my tears. The release brought incredible healing.

Annie openly shares some of her struggles as a worship intercessor. She grew up singing hymns with her mother and listening to Christian songs on tape. Music was the way she and God communed; He even woke her in the middle of the night with songs for herself and others. Wherever she went, people waited to hear God speak through one of her anointed songs, or charge the room with music as she strummed away on her guitar. Music became her identity. She loved it—even more than God. Then one day the music stopped.

Annie entered a long, lonely wilderness. For five stark years she sought the Lord in silence. But it was during that lengthy season of stripping that the Lord gave her an even greater gift— Himself. Annie tells it in her own words:

> The gift became more important than the Giver; I had actually begun to worship the worship. Pride had subtly crept in and music was where I found my sense of importance. It was in the wilderness that I laid my guitar upon His altar. He became my portion—my whole reason for living, even without the music. I no longer say that I will give God the glory; I don't want to touch it at all! Today when I sing, it is because He has put the burden there. It is His song, not mine. My heart is simply a holding tank for the music He wants to pour out upon the people.

Pitfalls of Worship Intercessors

Like Annie, all worship intercessors should guard their hearts to ensure that the *presents* of worship do not overshadow His *presence* in worship. The tendency to put the gift before the Giver is but one of the pitfalls that camouflage the pathway to purity in worship intercession. Others include:

- Fearing the response of others more than God's call to respond
- Refusing to move out in the anointing because of comparison
- Trying to make everyone happy and thereby worshiping to please the people rather than the Lord
- Allowing people to press for more than what God called for so that the worship becomes a sing-a-long rather than a cry of intercession
- Succumbing to rejection when the worship is not honored as a form of intercession
- Believing that only those with perfect pitch are anointed
- Lacking discernment in timing
- Becoming so excited about being recognized that the flesh takes over
- Thinking the voice has to be warmed up; thus making performance more important than the attitude of the heart
- Feeling responsible for creating the tune that will undergird the words rather than letting the Holy Spirit provide all of the music
- Trying to set the stage with words rather than moving out into the gift

- Hoping to move into worship intercession without laying a foundation of worship
- Being unteachable and overstepping the boundaries of others
- Thinking that song is the only way to pray, and losing the balance
- Believing that singing always means worship has occurred

Hannah, a Profile in Worship Intercession

Even those with very little biblical awareness know of King David's reputation as a worship intercessor. Most of the psalms are attributed to his name. Therefore, we have chosen to profile Hannah, who is seldom spotlighted as an example of surrendered worship intercession. Her story echoes with identification for all who have known the spiritual highs and lows of delay and delight in God's presence.

The part of Hannah's story recorded within the first and second chapters of 1 Samuel tells us that she is a mom in waiting and waiting and waiting . . . and waiting. Hannah not only bears the cultural embarrassment of her day as a barren woman, but she also shoulders the enormous burden of sharing her husband with a jealous rival whose ever-increasing crop of children grows healthier by the year! Hannah could have become a bitter blamer; instead, she became a bountiful bloomer. Worship intercession made the difference!

The following are some of the lessons we have discovered from Hannah's story. We hope you will read it for yourself and find even more.

- Purify your heart and release those who hurt you.
- Accept the fact that even those who love you most will not be able to comfort the places in your heart that are reserved for God's touch.
- Let your expressions of worship be real and come from the heart.
- Know that your motives in worship may be misunderstood—even by spiritual leaders—but don't soak in a tub of offense.
- Receive the blessings of others; allow God to speak to you through His leaders.
- Realize that worship intercession rehearses God's faithfulness, not people's failures.
- Be passionate rather than passive in your worship intercession.
- Understand that the waiting room is a lonely place only until you enter into God's presence; trust God to meet you there.
- If you are in a holding pattern, hold on to the Word—wing it, sing it and fling it forth in faith!
- Be sure that all worship intercession magnifies God and brings greater dependence upon Him.
- Understand that worship is not a performance. True worship flows; it is not forced.
- Celebrate His holiness, knowing that the pure in heart will see Him.
- Believe that you are responsible for the intercession; He is responsible for the outcome.
- Trust that God sees and knows everything!
- Follow through with your promises; broken covenants block breakthroughs.
- Refrain from always having to be in motion—dancing,

clapping, relying on instruments and the arts—instead of surrendering the heart.

- Allow worship to water the seeds for future harvests.
- Give God the glory; don't touch it.
- Continue to worship, even after the first signs of breakthrough appear, believing that God is a multiplier of miracles.
- Write down the songs of worship you receive—Hannah's song in 1 Samuel 2:1-10 is a reminder that they could be published.

Hannah's song of gratitude later became the prototype for Mary's song of praise in Luke 1:46-55, which is also known as the "Magnificat." What further proof do we need to realize that the praises of today can become a legacy for tomorrow's miracles? Though all other forms of intercession will eventually outlive their usefulness, worship's intercession will resound within the throne room forever and ever and ever!

It's about time we got started!

PERSONAL REFLECTION

Are You a Worship Intercessor?

1. Do you often sing your prayers or use a musical instrument to commune with the Lord?
2. Do you give either all or just a few bars of a song in response to a prayer request?
3. Does praising the Lord occupy much of your prayer time?
4. Does God give you a song to sing over a person, situation or land?

5. Do you wake up with a song on your heart?
6. When the group is asked if anyone has a song, can you usually say yes?

CHAPTER 10

GOVERNMENT INTERCESSORS

WATCHMEN FOR POLITICS AND CHURCH

"One day while the Civil War was raging at its worst, a minister said to President Abraham Lincoln, 'I surely hope the Lord is on our side.' To which Lincoln replied, 'I am not at all concerned about that, for I know that the Lord is always on the side of the right; but it is my constant anxiety and prayer that I and this nation should be on the Lord's side.'"[1]

The purpose of government intercessors is to stand on God's side as watchmen over political and church governments that represent the various countries, states, cities, neighborhoods, homes, schools and churches upon the earth. The Greek philosopher Aristotle wrote, "The state comes into existence that man may live. It continues that man may live well." But man can only live well when God is in control.

Godly governments empower people; conversely, ungodly

governments use their power to oppress people. Lord Acton said, "Power tends to corrupt and absolute power corrupts absolutely."[2] We agree, and we can think of no one who more adequately exemplifies an absolutely corrupt present-day leader than Saddam Hussein. Who can forget the memorable Wednesday night in January 1991, when television viewers of nearly every civilized nation worldwide watched with astonishment as the Gulf War unfolded before our very eyes?! The war appeared to be a struggle over Kuwait's crude oil. Oil, however, is symbolic of power, both physically and spiritually.

As this Middle Eastern megalomaniac hurled braggadocios in the face of America, a Christian nation, what he did not count on was that God's people would gather throughout the land to pray. Not unlike the prideful Goliath, Hussein's puffed chest deflated in a swift defeat that rendered him the laughingstock of the entire world. God honors the prayers of His government intercessors!

A Global Canopy of Prayer

"If God is so concerned about the nations," people ask, "then why are poor people in so many countries starving to death and living in complete chaos or ruin?" The answer is prayerlessness.

There are more than 6 billion people upon the earth and 188 United Nations member states in the world. In America alone, upwards of 109 million people currently profess to be born-again Christians.[3] Imagine what could happen if just 1 percent of those believers were to pray for the unsaved governments of the world! Edmund Burke said, "The only thing necessary for the triumph of evil is for good men to do nothing."[4] For years, *National Geographic* magazine and other forms of media have aided the Christian community by presenting photojournalism and news coverage about nations that have not yet heard the gospel. Most of us, however, have been impervious and invested little time interceding for them.

When the Lord issues a burden to pray and we respond in stubborn silence, we become Jonahs of prayer and defectors of the call. Jesus is Peace, and any nation that does not know Him cannot know peace. He said, "Peace be with you; as the Father has sent Me, I also send you" (John 20:21). He gave us His peace to first change the way we govern our own minds and then to send us, if only on our knees, to the people and nations of the world that also need to understand His government of peace.

The Lord insists that we can change a nation with our intercession. In 2 Chronicles 7:14 we read:

If my people, who are called by my name, will humble themselves and pray and seek my face and turn from their wicked ways, then will I hear from heaven and will forgive their sin and *will heal their land (NIV,* italics added).

This verse in 2 Chronicles is a call to the government intercessors of the Church. God can and will heal the lands of the earth if we are faithful to pray. The Bible assures us that before His return, the gospel will have been preached in every nation of the world (see Matt. 24:14). But before we can reach uncharted regions as foot soldiers, we must first have an army of pray-ers who will travel on their knees. Ministries such as the World Prayer Center in Colorado Springs, Colorado, are working day and night to make global prayer a reality.

Churches with a global focus are also emerging throughout the nations. (They are often identified by the flags draping from their ceilings as a reminder to prayerfully reach the unreached.)

Other people with a global consciousness are also being called to the forefront—ministries such as WIN (Window International Network), with a prayer focus on the 10/40 Window; Global Harvest Ministries, with a focus on the 40/70 Window; Every Home for Christ, with a focus on global missions. The call to missions from groups such as Youth With A Mission (YWAM) is more appealing to the youth of today than in any previous generation. This global mind-set points to one thing: the imminent return of Jesus Christ—the One of whom Isaiah prophesied, "The government will rest on His shoulders; and His name will be called Wonderful Counselor, Mighty God, Eternal Father, Prince of Peace" (Isa. 9:6).

Upholding the Bride, Christ's Church

The gallant King of kings and loving Lord of lords will soon burst through the heavenlies clothed in glory with radiant joy as He lifts the veil from the face of His pure and unblemished Bride, the Church (see 1 Tim. 6:15; Rev. 17:14; 19:7). At that moment, the prayers of all the ages past and present will culminate in heaven and Earth's long-awaited kiss. Until that time, however, many will be summoned to prayerfully attend to the Church.

Prayer is the greatest gift you can give
to a church, especially to your pastor.

Prayer is the greatest gift you can give to a church, especially to your pastor. If Church intercessors truly understood their place of importance, the whole congregation would reap the benefit of their sacrifice. When a pastor falls, part of the blame is shared with the congregation because we are the prayer shields for our leaders. We need to pray for the holiness and wholeness of their love for both God and His children.

It is said that every child goes through what are called oedipal days—times when a child falls innocently in love with the parent of the opposite sex. The reason for the infatuation is so the child will have an imprint stamped on his or her brain of the kind of person he or she is to marry. Using this analogy, pastors need our prayers so that their love for God's children will imprint on their lives the purity of Christ's love for them. Christians who have seen the holiness of God's love in their pastors will long for the love of Christ themselves! On the other hand, leaders who become confused and twisted by satanic deception and lust turn innocence into what is called an oedipal complex. Infatuation becomes lasciviousness; and not only does the child of God suffer, but so does the rest of the family.

Ministries are now springing up to bring healing to leaders who have fallen sexually, financially and in other ways. But we can help to prevent this problem by assembling members in the congregation to form a hedge of protection around every echelon of church leadership. Pastors with a minimum of two or three pray-ers interceding over every service exhibit a renewed strength in their teaching and preaching. Those who have enlisted personal intercessors are reporting greater fruitfulness in every facet of their lives, including their own holiness. We know this because personal intercessors are an important part of the service that Intercessors International provides.

Churches that have large congregations now report success in recruiting ministry teams to pray over the various branches within the church: choir, youth, missions, evangelism and outreaches. Numerous ministries have formed prayerwalking teams to regularly prayerwalk the neighborhoods and grounds around their church facilities. Others are calling organizations such as Intercessors International to send in teams of prayer support during citywide events and conferences.

Some leaders are even dropping their denominational guard to extend the love of Christ to other churches in regularly attended prayer vigils. As the walls of fear are crumbling in the Church, the walls of protection are rising in cities, counties and states, bringing renewed hope for the nation and our world.

Mama's Army of Intercessors

For many years, the late Dolores Hayford (known to most as Mama Hayford) led a weekly group called Gideons, at Church On The Way, that prayed for global, national, state and county government and church leaders by name. Mama Hayford scoured the media for governmental concerns that deserved concerted prayer. She researched significant legislative officials and assigned those leaders to the army of intercessors that congregated weekly under her assemblage to pray. Nations that suffered desolation or catastrophes of any kind were also brought before the Lord in prayer. On a local level, intercessory teams were dispatched into the various districts within the county of Los Angeles to prayer-drive the political turf. Every government building, church and school in that county was saturated in prayer.

Schools were a very important issue at the Gideons prayer meetings because, as Mama Hayford pointed out, the students of today are the leaders—in government and elsewhere—of tomorrow. Though Madalyn Murray O'Hair, the ACLU and other groups rallied support to keep prayer out of schools, the truth remains that almost every ancient civilization can in some way trace its educational roots to its religious beliefs and philosophers.

Moses, for example, was trained by the Egyptian priests in Pharaoh's court; he in turn took those skills to the Hebrews. Greeks studied under moral philosophers such as Socrates and Aristotle. The Chinese attribute their educational system to the teachings of Confucious, another moral philosopher. Much of the world has been educated by missionaries and organizations such as the International Bible Society, which has sent God's Word and other educational materials to the nations.

Few people reflect on the fact that, for a long time, the primer of American education was the Bible. The Pilgrim fathers of the United States did not settle in this nation because of its material wealth; they settled here to pursue their convictions about God—and they perpetuated those convictions through education! The pendulum to separate church and state has swung too far and is destroying our nation. Only prayer can change its course.

In the words of a student from Columbine High School in Littleton, Colorado:

The paradox of our time in history is that we have taller buildings but shorter tempers; wider freeways but narrower viewpoints; we spend more but have less; we buy more but enjoy it less. We have bigger houses but smaller families; more conveniences but less time; we have more

degrees but less sense; more knowledge but less judgment; more experts but more problems; more medicine
but less wellness.

We have multiplied our possessions but reduced our
values. We talk too much, love too seldom and hate too
often. We've learned how to make a living but not a life;
we've added years to life, not life to years.

We've been all the way to the moon and back but
have trouble crossing the street to meet the new neighbor. We've conquered outer space but not inner space;
we've cleaned up the air but polluted the soul. We've
split the atom but not our prejudice; we have higher
incomes but lower morals. We've become long on quan-
tity but short on quality. These are the times of tall men
and short character; steep profits and shallow relationships. These are the times of world peace but domestic
warfare; more leisure but less fun; more kinds of food
but less nutrition. These are days of two incomes but
more divorce; of fancier houses but broken homes.[5]

You may be a parent wondering whether your prayers can make
a difference. Begin by praying for the government in your home.
Talk to God about the things that need to change and allow Him
to change the hearts of those involved. Proverbs 21:1 says, "The
king's heart is like channels of water in the hand of the LORD; He
turns it wherever He wishes." The "king" refers to the person
who is governing the situation.

The things that happen where you live will have a lot to do
with how you, your family and others govern their lives. The
prophet Jeremiah explained, "And seek the welfare of the city
where I have sent you into exile, and pray to the LORD on its
behalf; for in its welfare you will have welfare" (Jer. 29:7). In other

words, if you want to be blessed where you live, be a blessing to that place.

God may be calling you to be a government intercessor by giving you the specifics to pray for a teacher in your child's classroom. You may be called to pray over the policies that will affect the school district in which you live. Start with what you know and what you see. As you are faithful to pray over even the least significant-looking governmental issue, God will broaden your prayer power. God is not looking for powerful speakers; He is looking for speakers who will rely on His power to speak up and speak out. Who knows? You could be a voice for God that will change the government!

World Events: Intercessors Behind the Scenes (and the Curtain)

One of the most celebrated events of our time happened on June 12, 1987, when President Ronald Reagan stood on a podium at the Berlin Wall and demanded, "Mr. Gorbachev, tear down this wall!" In a bold move that astounded the world, Reagan used his presidential bully pulpit to advocate a monumental change. What many people do not realize about this historic event is that it was preceded by much prayer. Behind the scenes, powerful intercessors such as Kjell Sjöberg, Dick Eastman, Jobst Bittner, Berthold Becker and others prayed on-site to tear down the spiritual walls before they actually crumbled.

Also behind the scenes, the Polish Pope John Paul II, who understood Communism intimately, used his influence in international political circles to agitate for freedom of religion and respect for the individual. A man of deep personal piety, we have to assume that John Paul II's prayers ascended to the Father on behalf of all believers oppressed by Communism.

Moreover, let us not forget about anonymous members of the various Orthodox and underground churches who for 40 years persevered on their knees in prayer behind the Iron Curtain, which hung for 70 years. Some of those faithful prayer warriors lived to see their prayers answered—their long nightmare finally over. One has to wonder, *Did they all really believe they would ever see it happen?*

The night the wall came down, Christians were there to pray and distribute Bibles, which were eventually placed in the hands of disarmed East German soldiers. Surely God uses government intercessors to change the political landscape of the world!

The Workplace, Our Mission Field for Change

God has His government intercessors tucked away in various cities, counties, states, nations, schools and churches around the globe. Some recognize that they have been placed there by God's providence, but few have seen all the ramifications of their intercession. Denny Fitzpatrick, for example, is a genial kind of guy that few people know, but one whose life has transformed city governments because he has whacked his way through the political jungles of spiritual warfare in prayer.

Denny, a manager of a well-known hotel chain, has used his job as a platform for impacting the city. He began by discreetly prayerwalking the building, lobby, halls, parking lot and finally the streets surrounding the hotel. We'll let Denny tell it:

In 1997, when I initially assumed the management position in Pasadena, California, I aligned in prayer agreement with other brothers and sisters to cover the more than 400,000 people who visited the hotel yearly. The employees began to see that something dynamic was happening. Staff members started asking questions and, before long, some were in my office surrendering their lives to Christ.

In Acts 1:8, Jesus said, "You shall receive power when the Holy Spirit has come upon you; and you shall be My witnesses both in Jerusalem, and in all Judea and Samaria, and even to the remotest part of the earth." For me, Jerusalem meant the hotel (my workplace), and the atmosphere really did begin to buzz with the power of the Holy Spirit. But I knew God was also calling me to a Judea and a Samaria.

I joined a group of intercessors who faithfully gathered to intercede for the city. We prayed for the local fire stations, police departments, schools, churches and other government-related facilities; we even called many of them and asked for prayer requests. Twenty-one churches and ministries eventually joined our group, along with numerous local political representatives.

The change in our Judea became evident rather quickly. Crime decreased and churches began to burst forth with robust power. During that time, our potent group of intercessors was literally burying Bibles in the city's soil as a prophetic act to multiply God's Word in the land; we also proclaimed God's truths from the top of the tower at City Hall. We prayerwalked on our lunch breaks and sought the input of Dr. C. Peter Wagner from Global Harvest Ministries, who offered strategies that were later implemented.

Today, I manage another enormous hotel for the same chain in Spokane, Washington. When I first arrived here, the place was in a spiritually deplorable state and stood on the brink of financial despair. But God had other plans! The hotel has now attained its highest profit in more than eight years. I have aligned with local churches and another strong group of intercessors here who are currently bringing Christ to this Samaria. We have already sectioned off the city on a prayer map and are sending prayerwalkers out two-by-two each week. Government officials in our town are prayed for by name and those supplications are making a difference.

Because the nations are Jesus' inheritance, we must sow seed into governmental soil so He can reap a harvest. By changing a city, we change a state; and who knows how that state will affect the nation! We know we can't change the world by ourselves, but we have aligned with Jesus, the only One who can. The spiritual warfare here has been tremendous, but we've read the final chapter of God's History Book and we know the ultimate outcome:

WE WIN!

Government Intercessor? Not Me!

We win when every person in the Church finds his or her designated place in prayer. One of the first experiences the Lord used to make me (Beth) aware of the different prayer anointings happened on a trip to Washington, DC, during the primary years of my Christian walk. I agreed to accompany a friend who was part of a women's group that gathered daily to pray on Capitol Hill. These tenacious intercessors battled on their spiritual knees for the various bills brought to the floor.

Intercession was prompted by the announcement that a particular bill was coming up for a vote. The women would then pray for the various lawmakers, reminding the Lord how each lawmaker had voted previously and petitioning Him to align their hearts with heaven's righteousness. They cried out for the scales to be removed from bureaucratically blind eyes and rambled on and on about details of the bill until they sensed that the bill and the man had melded together in God's will. The more they prayed, the more my conscience rebuffed me; I was overwhelmed with guilt. I still remember thinking, *This country is going down the drain and it's all my fault! I don't understand a thing they're talking about—and even worse, I don't care. This is like a foreign language that I have no desire to learn. It's way beyond my comprehension.*

I left for home cloaked in feelings of condemnation. When I finally met with the heavenly Father alone, I asked, "Lord, what am I going to do?"

His answer jolted me: "Stick within the sphere of your anointing!" I didn't fully understand what He was talking about, so I pressed on in prayer until I heard, "If there is a crisis, I will call you to pray for the nations. And if there if a crisis for a man in the nation, I will call you to pray. Your job is to lift up the hands of the leaders of the nations as I place them on your heart."

There is no way to describe the freedom those words brought or the magnitude of the release I felt from the bondage of having to share the same passion as the women I had met on Capitol Hill. You see, it wasn't only that I didn't have a clue what those women were talking about that made me feel so guilty—it was that I didn't care! I now realize that it is the Lord who places the burden on our hearts. If He wants you or me to carry a burden, He will give us a passion to do so.

⚭

I now realize it is the Lord who places the burden on our hearts. If He wants you or me to carry a burden, He will give us a passion to do so.

⚭

You might not be a person who can pray over a daily list for the leaders in your church, your schools or your city, state or national government. You might be a crisis intercessor who is called to respond to governmental kinds of emergencies. On the other hand, maybe you don't hear heaven's SOSs for leaders. That's okay! You need only know what place God is calling you to in prayer. Simply ask the Lord where you have been anointed to stand with His prayer power and He will show you. The important point is this: Find your place and stick with it until God gives you new orders!

PITFALLS OF GOVERNMENT INTERCESSORS

One possible pitfall among government intercessors can be intolerance for those who appear ignorant about governmental matters. Others include:

- Becoming so concerned about the government that people become a secondary issue—and so does the Lord
- Allowing recognition to be the motive for intercessory prayer rather than a call of God
- Compromising integrity and beliefs to please people
- Getting caught up in the spirits that are over the land, which are power and pride
- Taking offense when convictions are questioned
- Believing that you're the only one with the answer
- Letting bitterness take root when leaders do not live up to God's will
- Gossiping and grumbling about leaders instead of leading them into change through prayer

DANIEL, A PROPHETIC GOVERNMENT INTERCESSOR

Daniel's gripping biography lucidly illustrates the strength of character necessary for government intercessors. Abducted as a teen when Babylon's King Nebuchadnezzar besieged Jerusalem, Daniel was recruited—along with three of his closest prayer partners—into government. Why Daniel? The Bible explains that he was from nobility and "handsome, showing aptitude for every kind of learning, well informed, quick to understand, and qualified to serve in the king's palace" (Dan. 1:4, *NIV*).

Like Daniel, government intercessors are those who do not forget their noble spiritual roots, no matter who governs the environment in which they live or work. They know the importance of partnering with others in prayer, and have teachable, discerning spirits.

When Daniel and his friends arrived in Babylon, their names were changed to reflect the pagan gods of that government. They were also immediately enrolled in the Babylonian educational system so that they might learn the language and embrace the polytheism of that land. Even then, church, government and schools were an inseparable three-strand cord.

Through the lives of these four godly men we discover the cornerstone of success in government intercession: uncompromising convictions. Godly convictions are those things we are willing to be convicted for—whether that means being unfairly called a "con" and tossed into a fiery furnace or eaten alive in a lion's den. The cost for representing God's government includes an almost certain consequence of being mistreated, misrepresented and mistaken among those we are praying for.

A Tale of Two Lions

The book of Daniel gives an incredible study of two kinds of lions. The first is the Lion of Judah (see Rev. 5:5); Daniel represents this lion. Proverbs 28:1 says that "the righteous are bold as a lion." Lions do not beg; they aggressively pursue their portion. When we have sought God for His will and put our confidence in His desire to provide, we boldly and aggressively lay hold of our portion in prayer.

Conversely, the Bible says that there is also a counterfeit lion. In 1 Peter 5:8 we are told that the devil, "prowls about like a roaring lion, seeking someone to devour." Notice the word "like." He does not have the power of the Lion of Judah; he only imitates that power. He is a rebel lion—in other words, a counterfeit that has been spawned out of rebellion. The sorcerers and other workers of witchcraft in the book of Daniel (see 2:2; 4:7; 5:11) represent the rebel lions, but they don't stand a chance when the righteous take their place in prayer.

We recommend that every government intercessor read the book of Daniel. The following are only some of the lessons we have gleaned. We hope you will plumb the depths of this incredible book and discover even more.

- Appeal to the chain of command, even if those in authority are ungodly, but do not break God's laws.
- Honor God in your prayer closet and He will honor you publicly.
- Put your trust in God's ability to change people's hearts rather than in your own eloquence.
- Expect your convictions to be tested.
- Watch your appetite and don't feast on things that are delicacies at Satan's table—pride, lust, materialism and celebrity!
- Be accepting of ungodly people without embracing ungodly convictions.
- Get the facts before you pray for leaders and governments.
- Come into agreement with godly prayer partners before you speak up and speak out on government or church issues.
- Allow God to provide His "super" wisdom before you bring discernment to the "superman," or leader.
- Give God the credit for the discernment you receive.
- Don't discount your dreams or the dreams of others until you have sought the Lord for their interpretation.
- Realize that truth will always be refined in a fiery furnace of trial and people are watching to see if God is in the fire with you.

- Know that the furnace will be hotter than what was anticipated, but it will not burn you up—it will only make you shine brighter!
- Accept the fact that it takes time to earn the confidence of leaders.
- Trust in God's restorative power, even when the leaders around you are acting like animals.
- Ask God to interpret "the handwriting on the wall" for leaders who are walking outside of His will.
- Believe that no country is impenetrable and that prosperity without godliness is a guarantee for destruction, so pray for wisdom rather than wealth.
- Allow your legacy to rest in the hands of God.
- Count the cost of compromise before the cost counts you.
- Don't judge a son by the righteousness of his father; let each man's works be judged on their own merit.
- Keep your prayer windows open and expect to be attacked for your faith.
- Refuse the lie that you have nothing to contribute in your old age; let the latter years be the most productive years.
- Realize that the lion's den is where your faith will be stripped to the bone but witnessed by all.
- Don't take vengeance into your own hands (see Rom. 12:19).
- Pray and fast for a spirit of identificational repentance for your enemies.
- Believe that your prayer is heard the moment you speak it and that warfare in the heavenlies may delay your answer, but can't stop it.
- Trust God for revelation and details in all that concerns your prayer life.

Government intercessors are the spiritual Daniels of our day. They are the ones who will see "the handwriting on the wall" and know how to pray accordingly. That prayer effort might be for a family, a church, a neighborhood, a school, a city, a state, a nation or many nations. The key is to stand like Daniel with a disciplined focus at the windows of prayer.

If you refuse to bow to the rebel lion, your final bow before the Lion of Judah will be greatly rewarded!

PERSONAL REFLECTION
ARE YOU A GOVERNMENT INTERCESSOR?

1. Do politics stimulate you?
2. Does your life revolve around the church?
3. Are you interested in policies for schools, churches and political situations?
4. Would prayerwalking the schools, churches and government buildings in your neighborhood excite you?
5. Are you called to intercession for your government as you read the newspaper or watch global news?
6. Do you keep apprised of government officials by name in any level of government?

Notes
1. Walter B. Knight, *Knight's Master Book of New Illustrations* (Grand Rapids, MI: Wm. B. Eerdmans Publishing Company, 1956), p. 463.
2. John Bartlett, *Bartlett's Familiar Quotations* (Boston, MA: Little, Brown & Company, 1980), p. 615, no. 15.
3. Website: http:www.barna.org/cgi-bin/MainArchives.asp.
4. Bartlett, p. 374, no. 12.
5. This quote was sent to me by a friend and is taken from a widely publicized and circulated e-mail on the Internet. The author is anonymous.

CHAPTER 11

PEOPLE-GROUP AND ISRAEL INTERCESSORS

PRAYER SHEPHERDS FOR ETHNIC GROUPS

"Ubiquitous!" The word means everywhere at the same time. God is ubiquitous. He is everywhere at all times in spirit upon the earth, but He has also limited Himself physically to being wherever we go as ambassadors of His love. As heaven's royal representatives who have been spiritually robed in Christ's loving authority, we are called to roll up our spiritual sleeves and wear out the knees of our prayer fatigues for the billions of people who do not know Him.

The Bible says that without Jesus, we are like sheep without a shepherd (see Mark 6:34). To survive in the world, people, like sheep, need (1) a shepherd to care for them, (2) others to follow, and (3) a place of belonging. Because sheep are by nature dumb and defenseless, their safety is found in groups, as is ours.

Clearly, birds of a feather flock together, but they do so for the sake of protection. Therefore, by prayerfully "penetrating people groups," or whole flocks of people, with God's love, countless numbers are finding true security and protection in Christ.

Two Groups, One God

The term "people groups" can refer to any group of people based on background, status, residence, occupation, health, knowledge, religion, race, nationality—the list could be endless. As we target a group of people in prayer, God will surface unlikely leaders within the group whom He can use to turn it around. Lambs don't follow the shepherd, they follow the sheep that follow the shepherd. In other words, as we show others the way, they will eventually lead herds of others along that same path.

When all people everywhere have finally heard the gospel, the world will be sorted into only two groups: those going to heaven and those going to hell (see Matt. 25:32,33). It is not our job to sort the sheep; it is our job to lead them in by following the Shepherd. One of the ways we lead is through prayer.

The Lord said, "The effective prayer of a righteous man [or woman] can accomplish much" (Jas. 5:16). But what is effective prayer? We believe it is prayer that follows after the heart of the Good Shepherd, Jesus. The shortest sermon He ever preached was, "Follow Me" (see Matt. 9:9; Mark 2:14; Luke 5:27). When this succinct sermon is fully observed by all, including the people-group intercessors throughout the earth, the whole world will assuredly be evangelized. John Wesley put it this way: "I look upon all the world as my parish." We are called to love all the people of the world because God does.

Notice that we use the term "love." Strong-arming, condemning and driving people into the Kingdom will only provoke them to defensiveness and cause them to avoid us. We must talk to God about people before we ever talk to people about God. Saint Augustine taught that we are to preach the gospel with our lives and only when necessary use words—that kind of evangelism is learned by staying very close to the Shepherd in prayer.

Finding a Focus

God has countless ways of focusing our attention on the group or groups we are to prayerfully and demonstrably affect. He may allow us to walk into a difficult circumstance where a people group we never thought we could love will become part of our lives. For example, Charles Colson, special counsel to President Richard Nixon during Watergate, descended from a place of political prestige into a state penitentiary. There Colson met Christ and later founded Prison Fellowship, a ministry that both physically and prayerfully continues to change a people group—American prisoners and their families.

As with Dr. Martin Luther King, Jr., the Lord may use our racial hurts to become the platform for praying for others and impacting their lives. Dr. King did not stumble over his sorrows or whine about the deep-rooted pain of prejudice; he prayed and sought God for a plan that would forever elevate his people group among the nations. His noble legacy will be celebrated throughout history.

Satan may wound us through a people group. And yet, if we pray, the Lord will redeem our hurts and allow us to lead our enemies to Christ. The chronicles of Corrie ten Boom provide story after story of God's redemptive love. Corrie's family died in the Ravensbruck prison camp for hiding and transporting Jews during the Nazi Holocaust, but she surrendered those hurts to God and became a messenger of His forgiveness to post-war Europe. The poignant recounting in *The Hiding Place* of Corrie's hesitant hand reaching forth in forgiveness to the officer responsible for her sister's death and her own abusive degradation challenges each of us to unconditionally love our enemies. Her words of reconciliation have become a healing balm for the fragmented and fractured hearts of victims everywhere.

You may think these examples extreme; that's okay. God may use a timely sermon to tug at your heart and call your attention to a people group that needs your prayer. He may place a book in your lap that will summon your interest and compel you to prayerfully drop to your knees. You need only ask and He will direct you to the group that most needs your intercession and loving acts of kindness.

A Wake-Up Call

When the Lord has an assignment for you, He knows your address and He will seek you out to deliver it. Jean Steffenson, for example, was sovereignly sought out by God to lift up the American Indians because she identifies with God's heart, has surrendered her will and sacrificially serves His kingdom. In 1987, God paid Jean a visit. Let's read the story from her perspective.

I've been an intercessor since 1972, and my whole desire since then has been to know God's will and what is on His heart so that the Holy Spirit can energize my prayers. For 15 years I had interceded for America as a nation. Then one morning in 1987, at about 5 A.M., I was awakened by a holy presence that flooded my unlit bedroom. I asked, "God, what is on Your heart?"

Suddenly, my own deep pangs of sorrow broke the hushed silence. My weeping turned to groaning and continued until nearly 2 P.M. I knew the Lord was grieved and was birthing His burden through me. I called a pastor for prayer. Later, the Lord gave me a vision of a dark canopy covering the Church of America; it was tightly secured from underneath by something grotesque. "God," I inquired, "what is that?"

He explained, "It represents the atrocities committed against the first people of this land."

When I asked what I should believe Him for, He answered, "Believe that the first people of this land will be healed, take their place in the Church of America and go to the nations as My ambassadors."

"Lord," I asked, "what do you want *me* to do?" He told me to pray. You see, God is a God of nations. He judges nations and He judges between nations. The word "nations" is literally *ethnos,* from which we get the word "ethnic." In other words, God judges the way one ethnic group treats another. But because God is mercy, before He judges anything, He will look for an intercessor to pray. We see this clearly in Isaiah 59. Then, in Genesis 19, Abraham, God's first intercessor, was called to pray for mercy over the cities of Sodom and Gomorrah because God longed to extend mercy to those people. In James 2:13 we read, "Mercy triumphs over judgment."

When God gives the call, He confirms it by endowing us with mercy and causing us to identify with the people group He is laying upon our heart. From 1987 to 1992, I prayed for the Native American *ethnos,* of which there are more than 300 federally recognized tribes. After five years of private intercession, the Lord showed me that I was to go public with the things upon His heart. When God asks us to intercede, generally He will allow us to become part of the answer to our prayers. He had rallied a team of intercessors to support me in carrying this burden, so together we set out to make His heart known.

In 1992, we planned a corporate prayer meeting, which we referred to as a reconciliation ceremony, in downtown Denver, Colorado—the site of a scathing injustice against the American Indians who formerly possessed that land. There, we repented for the Sand Creek Massacre, which you can read about in John Dawson's brilliant book *Healing America's Wounds.* Leaders from various tribal governments, city and state legislatures, and churches, as well as many other Christians, stood with the 150 in attendance on that chilly morning.

Because the Sand Creek Massacre erupted with the cold-blooded clenched fist of a Methodist minister, church leaders were first in humbling themselves before tribal chiefs, beseeching their forgiveness. The flood-gates of reconciliation opened wide and an outpouring of healing now continues to wash the infection of bitterness that once maligned the dignity of local tribes.

The Lord continues to broaden the call. What began

as a call to prayer became a lifestyle of intercession. Love is what qualifies this lifestyle. But the love must start with a commitment to God and not the people. My love for the people flows out of my love for God. The Lord is my focus, and answering His heart's cry is my mission. If you or I go to a wounded people group expecting recognition or gratitude, we set ourselves up for disappointment. But if we lay our lives down for the things on God's heart, no sacrifice is too great or too difficult.

We can rest assured that our intercession cannot be silenced—not even by the grave. The prayers of the martyrs echo throughout the hallways of time.

COUNTING THE COST

The call to intercession is costly. It may be followed by a summons to occupy a hostile environment where the altars of satanic gods have wrought the curse of idolatry upon the land and its people groups. It may even cost us our lives. But regardless of the repercussions, we can rest assured that our intercession cannot be silenced—not even by the grave. The prayers of the martyrs echo throughout the hallways of time. And though Satan has blinded the eyes of people within every nation, believers in Jesus

Christ are penetrating even the fiercest strongholds with the truth about His love for them.

I (Karen) have a plaque above my desk inscribed with a quote from Hudson Taylor, missionary to China. It says: "It is possible to sing, 'My all is on the altar,' and yet be unprepared to sacrifice a ring from one's finger, or a picture from one's wall, or a child from one's family for the salvation of the heathen." Some of us live in countries that are very wealthy, yet we struggle to fast one meal for the unsaved or sacrifice 10 minutes of entertainment to pray for the persecuted people groups around the world.

In their gripping book *The Move of the Holy Spirit in the 10/40 Window*, Luis Bush and Beverly Pegus reveal compelling stories of people who have literally laid down all to serve Christ. They point to Sudanese Christians as one of the most persecuted people groups in the world, with documented stories to back up their claims. But they also share the positive side of persecution and the need for forgiveness. Let's read it together:

This Sudanese brother said something I (Beverly) will never forget. He wanted us to pray not that persecution would stop but that believers would continue to be empowered by God to share the Gospel everywhere they were scattered! I remember feeling amazed and challenged as I listened to his words. I questioned myself: Would the Lord find me this faithful if I were persecuted in this way? I prayed that He would.

I learned one of life's most important lessons during a trip overseas in 1997 when we met together with some students to pray. What the students shared with us broke our hearts. We knew about Sudan's refugee camps—called "human zoos"—where Christian families were forced to renounce their faith in Jesus Christ in order to feed themselves and their children. We were told that the children in the camps were starving to death and only a thin layer of skin covered their little skeletons. We wept when one of the students told us how his mother was tied up and placed in the middle of the floor while Muslims repeatedly stabbed his brother until he died in front of her eyes. His brother's crime: converting from Islam to Christianity!

They shared that there are more than 1 million Spirit-filled believers in Sudan. . . . I asked the Lord to reveal why so many Spirit-filled believers could not overcome the powers of darkness in their nation. . . . The next day the Lord showed us one of the keys to destroying demonic strongholds in persecuted nations and in the lives of people held in bondage.

During our next meeting with the students, we discussed the importance of forgiving, praying for, loving, and blessing our enemies; loving those who are persecuting us, and praying for those in authority over us. I commented, "If we do not pray the will of God, we aren't praying any differently than the witch doctors."

I heard a gasp. Then a quiet voice responded, "We haven't been praying the will of God."

The Lord prompted me to say, "You need to forgive, pray for, and love those who are committing these horrific atrocities against the people in your country." I asked them, "Do you pray for those who are in authority over you and for those who are persecuting the Christians in Sudan?"

They answered, "We pray for them, but not in the way you're talking about." The students admitted later that they had been praying "like the witch doctors" and not in the way the Lord commands us to pray as believers for our enemies and oppressors.

The Lord had answered my prayer and shown me one of the reasons the Church of Jesus Christ in Sudan was in bondage. They had been cursing their enemies instead of obeying the instructions from the Word of God to bless them; they had been hating their enemies instead of loving them; they had been praying for ungodly things to happen to those in authority over them instead of praying for their salvation (Matt. 5:44; Rom. 12:14).

When the students understood the hardness that unforgiveness had created in them, they repented (Matt. 6:14, 15). They went to the Word of God and prayed that the Lord would bring blessings and salvation to the Islamic regime. Then the students asked the Lord to soften their hearts to be able to love their enemies. As we prayed I saw a mental picture of a lock with a skeleton key. The key then entered the lock, and the Lord told me, "Forgiveness is one of the keys to changing the destiny of a persecuted nation."

The lesson we learned from these precious students is that no matter how terrible the things are that happen to us, we cannot allow them to fester in us. We must combat the sins of unforgiveness and hatred with Christ-empowered forgiveness. We must choose God's way, which is to forgive our enemies and pray according to the Word of God.[1]

The Jews and Israel

If it had not been for the Jews, none of us would have the Word of God today. God, as man, could have come through any people group of the world, but He chose to be born a Jew: "salvation is from the Jews" (John 4:22). The Jews are the forefathers of

Christianity; they gave us scribes who meticulously wrote the Bible—the prophetic calendar which gave us the promise of a messiah for all peoples. And they gave us our Savior Himself.

Three major monotheistic religions—Christianity, Judaism and Islam—dominate the world today. All have roots in Abraham, the Hebrew father of Ishmael and Isaac. Abraham fathered Ishmael through a surrogate mother (also called a concubine) named Hagar. He did so at the request of Sarah, his wife, who believed God had forgotten His promise to give her a son (see Gen. 16:2). But as He always does, God fulfilled His Word to Sarah. In her old age she bore Isaac in what she had suspected to be her post-childbearing 90s (see Gen. 15—18).

God had promised Abraham that he would become the "father of a multitude of nations" through Sarah (Gen. 17:4), but Hagar's son, Ishmael, was a constant reminder to Sarah of her inability to trust God. Consequently, she insisted that Hagar be put out; Abraham reluctantly agreed. The despondent Hagar migrated to the Arabian desert, where God promised that Ishmael would also be a great nation (see Gen. 21:18).

Today, Ishmael's descendants represent the Arab nations, most of which are Islamic and follow the teachings of Mohammed. The place where God spoke to Hagar is now an idolatrous shrine in Mecca known as the Kaaba, where Muslims, the observers of Islam, make their present-day pilgrimages. Ishmael settled for a false god while Isaac remained faithful to Jehovah, the one true God and Creator of all the nations.

A Promised People Group for a Promised Land

The world shares a common destiny with Israel and the Jews because the Jews are the people group Jehovah calls the apple of

His eye. He prophesied through Zechariah that the nations that plundered the Jews would pay for their deeds "for he who touches [Israel], touches the apple of His eye" (Zech. 2:8). The fulfillment of this prophecy has rung true throughout history. Dominant empires have been reduced to impotence for wounding those of whom the Lord spoke when He said, "Israel is My son, My first-born" (Exod. 4:22).

History reveals that the Hebrews are the descendants of Noah's son Shem from whom we get the term "Shemite" translated Semite (see Gen. 10:21). So to be anti-Semitic is usually thought to be against the Hebrews, or Jews. The term "Jew" is derived from the words "Judah" and "Judaism." Permit us to explain.

Much confusion exists over whether the Jews are a nation or a religion or one and the same. The fact is that Abraham's grandson Jacob, who later became known as Israel, fathered 12 sons that represent the 12 tribes of Israel, a nation or *ethnos* (ethnic group). The original 12 tribes migrated with Moses and Joshua to the Promised Land of Canaan, also known as Palestine. King David ruled that land and so did his son Solomon. But after Solomon's death, Canaan was divided, kind of like the division between the North and South in America's history. Ten tribes joined the North to become a state—they were called Israel; two tribes joined the South to become a state—they were called Judah. Unfortunately, in 722 B.C., Assyria wiped out the 10 tribes of Israel, so Judah became the remnant, or Judeans, Jewish people who observe Judaism.

PERSECUTED BUT PRESERVED

Probably no other people group in history has been more scattered or persecuted than the Jewish people. Though incomprehensible, we know that persecution has also added to their preservation. We would like you to hear Dennis Kaufman's thoughts on this subject because he is a Jewish believer in Jesus Christ:

> Like the sabra or cactus plant that grows in the desert of Israel, the Jews have walked through numerous desert experiences and have had to grow protective thorns to survive. I believe, however, that the Jewish people would have assimilated into the rest of the world if it had not been for the tremendous persecution they sustained, especially at the hands of professed Christians.
>
> Most Jews lump all people into two categories: Jews and goyim (non-Jews). In other words, one is either a Jew or an enemy of the Jew. They have, after all, suffered incredible persecution from not only Arabs but Christians as well—the Crusades, the Spanish Inquisition, Charlemagne's rule, the pogroms; ethnic cleansing and what I consider the clincher, the Nazi Holocaust.
>
> It is human nature to do everything possible to survive those who hate you. The Jews have been hated by just about everyone. They survive because they cling to each other. Many believe that to assimilate is to guarantee extinction.
>
> My grandfather taught me that anybody who was not a Jew was our enemy. My dad and my grandparents on both sides migrated from Russia after my aunt was killed in the pogrom. We lived in a predominantly Jewish neighborhood in New York. Then, in my first year at the University of Illinois, I was subjected to anti-Semitism. Because of the upheaval and unrest in Israel, somebody

painted "Alms to the Arabs, death to the Jews" on the steps of the school's library.

I returned to New York and graduated from New York University where a professor assured me that climbing a corporate ladder would only be possible if a Jew sat on the board of directors; I sought out a company with a Jewish CEO. Later, as a buyer for one of the largest shoe chains in America, I was asked to travel to the South for business. Occasionally, hotels, restaurants and country clubs posted signs that warned: "No Jews, No Negroes, No Dogs." I remember joking, "Well, at least we finally got top billing!" But anti-Semitism is no laughing matter, and neither is racism.

Now, as a believer in Jesus Christ, my wife and I speak to large audiences for a soul-winning ministry. The fact that any anti-Semitism still exists in the Church is grievous to my spirit. Our vocabularies need to be purged of phrases such as "Jew him down." I am not supersensitive to this problem, but I do know that it needs to be a matter of prayerful concern among believers. Jews have an almost instinctive discernment for the anti-Semitic spirit.

Jesus said that He came to bring the gospel message to the Jew first; but the fact that the Jew did not receive it has been a blessing to the Gentile nations, not a curse. The first branches of the Early Church were all Jewish; the Gentile nations were grafted into that Jewish family tree. Thus, by receiving the refused inheritance of Israel, Jesus' family tree now represents all nations—just what He was hoping for!

The battle to win "Israel, God's first-born" back to Christ must begin with prayer; it is a spiritual battle.

Pray that the scales will be removed from their eyes as they were for the Jewish apostle Paul in Acts 9. Pray that the roots of rejection and the scars of persecution will be healed. Most Jews feel rejected by God and man, and that rejection is fueled by an underlying fear of being hurt. Therefore, pray for your own peace and joy so that you will be able to reflect Jesus' peace to the Jews. Psalm 122 says to pray for the peace of Jerusalem because that is what the Jews are searching for—everlasting peace!

The Voice of Reconciliation

The Lord is raising up the voices of Gentile believers worldwide to reestablish the honor of His cherished Jewish remnant. We at Intercessors International find that in Germany, those who really love Jesus are now prayerfully standing in the gap for Israel and the Jewish people throughout the world.

An American pastor with German roots who is speaking out on behalf of Jewish people is Jim Goll, author of the informative *Father, Forgive Us*. We interviewed Jim for this book. The following paragraphs are some excerpts from that conversation:

Zechariah 12:3 says in essence that whoever picks up Jerusalem, picks up a heavy stone. Therefore, I want to speak a word of sobriety. Realize that the Scriptures do give a distinctive warning that when you start picking up this precious jewel called Jerusalem, which is close to the heart of God, you are picking up warfare—a time bomb! Every believer is called to pray for Israel's peace in a general way, just as 1 Timothy 2:1,2 calls us all to pray for those in authority over us. But there are also distinctive graces deposited and released in people to pray in a more focused way.

When you make a decision to pray for Israel and the Jews, sit down and count the cost, realizing that as you touch this stone, you touch one of the central prophetic purposes of God for all generations—and the devil does not like it! So before you touch this stone, be sure that you are obeying God's assignment and God's grace rather than falling into the trap of romanticism.

One of the primary Scriptures I bank on is Zechariah 12:10: "I will pour out on the house of David and on the inhabitants of Jerusalem . . ." Too often, the Church spiritualizes the contextual understanding of the promises that have been given to the Jewish people and lifts those promises out as though they were written exclusively for the Church. Though I do believe these promises also apply to the Church as spiritual Jews, it is wrong to inflate their application to the Church and forget the house of David or Jerusalem, the city for which they were intended.

So how do we pray for the house of David and the inhabitants of Jerusalem?

- Speak forth proclamations and the praises of spiritual warfare over them.
- Pray that miraculous signs and wonders will be released to them.
- Ask God to convict them of sin so they will see their need for a savior.
- Pray that the religious blinders or scales would fall off their eyes.

- Speak comfort to them to bind the wounds of persecution they have suffered.
- Ask for God's grace, recognizing that this Jewish stone will not be heavy for the ones who have been graced to carry it.

Do you want to become close to the things that are closest to God's heart? Do you want to love the things that God loves? Do you want to pray for things that Jesus is always interceding for at the Father's right hand? Then you will become an Israel prayer-aholic!

Prayer for the Workers

Numerous ministries are now prayerfully and tangibly helping to pick up the precious stone of Israel. International Christian Embassy Jerusalem (ICEJ) has a prayer house both in America and in Israel. This organization also leads a prayer journey in Jerusalem to celebrate the feast of tabernacles; Christians from around the world join in this annual prayer pilgrimage. The American Christian Trust in Washington, DC, is another ministry that pulsates with prayer for Israel. Some organizations are winning Israelis to Christ without a word by living in the land and distributing food and clothing there. For example, Bridges for Peace, which has satellite offices in America and Canada that pray and raise funds for Israel, now distributes more than 1,000 pounds of food daily to hungry Jewish refugees in that land.

There is a buzz of excitement in the heavenlies as all ethnic groups of the world are sensing the rumblings of revival. Never have so many Jewish people been more open to the gospel message of Jesus Christ than they are now. The Bible predicted that the first would be last and the last would be first (see Matt. 20:16). And so it is! Israel, God's firstborn, is returning home in record numbers as the Lord Himself is racing toward Jerusalem to wrap His arms around the prodigal and unveil the city's long-awaited Prince of Peace.

Trust is being reestablished. A Jewish lady recently shared her fear about trusting those who have persecuted her people group in the past: "Can a leopard change its spots?" she asked.

"No," I (Karen) replied, "but the One who created the leopard can!"

"*C*an a leopard change its spots?"
"No, but the One who created the leopard can!"

God can recreate hearts and minds and relationships that are wickedly spotted with the cancerous hatred of this world. We need only believe that His forgiveness is greater than our pain and allow Him to do the work!

Christians have been called to be bridges to the Muslim, to the Jew, to the Hindu, to the Buddhist, to the New Ager, to the homosexual, to the AIDS victim, to the prisoner, to the prosti-tute, to the gangbanger, to the addict, and to the lonely, home-less and downtrodden.

As bridges, we can expect to be walked on, used and asked to carry more than we ever thought possible. We will encounter those who are not like us and don't want to be. The tracks of many may scar us with hurtful impressions. But we are not asked to do or be in our own strength. Underneath us are the everlasting arms of the Bridge Creator between God and humans, heaven and Earth, time and eternity. He is the One who said, "With men this is impossible, but with God all things are possible" (Matt. 19:26). Ask Him what people group needs you—become the bridge of possibility that will lead them out of their impossible circumstances.

Pitfalls of People-Group and Israel Intercessors

Thinking that we can change people groups with our own strength is just one of the pitfalls that people-group and Israel intercessors will confront. Others include:

- Growing weary in well-doing because the focus is directed toward the people group rather than flowing out of a jubilant love for God
- Succumbing to resentment because of people's ingratitude
- Falling prey to hatred for opposers of the targeted people group
- Praying "witchcraft" prayers instead of love for the enemy of the people group
- Believing that persecution cannot benefit God's purpose
- Losing patience when nothing happens year after year
- Using prayer to manipulate, preach or muscle others rather than allowing the Holy Spirit to do the work

- Setting an agenda for God to follow in prayer rather than obeying His instructions to "follow Me"
- Picking up the stone of Jerusalem and forgetting that it brings with it warfare
- Looking at the assignment through the rose-colored lenses of romanticism (a religious spirit) rather than an assignment from God

The Woman at the Well, a Profile of the People-Group Intercessor

You will never meet a person or people group that Jesus does not love and did not die for, nor will you ever meet a person who has accumulated so much sin debt that Christ's blood cannot reverse it. You will never meet a person with a mask so convincing that God cannot see beyond it, nor will you ever meet a person who has been so exploited that God cannot cover the shame. You will never meet a person who sought God's mercy and did not find it in Christ, nor will you ever meet a person who refused Christ's mercy and did not forsake his or her own redemption.

Jesus Himself has never rejected anyone. In John 4, we see His unconditional acceptance of a woman who was a social outcast through both a polluted lifestyle and a polluted lineage. But Jesus looked beyond what she had done and where she came from to see who she could become. (Isn't that what He did with you and me?) Amazingly, God called a five-time loser, who had been flirting with life-threatening sin all of her adult life, and turned her into a mighty people-group intercessor.

When praying for a people group, we will find that, just as this woman seemed an unlikely candidate to understand the deeper things of God and lead others into that same revelation, God will place a heavenly thumbprint on someone you least expect—it could be you. Let's explore some of the lessons from this Samaritan woman's call to people-group intercession:

- Be alert to an encounter with Jesus, knowing that He will seek you out, even if you feel disqualified by a Samaritan heritage or a shattered reputation.
- Allow the shameful places in your past and present to be scrutinized and forgiven through an encounter with Jesus' holiness.
- Linger in His presence until you have received spiritual revelation before you ever attempt to meet the spiritual needs of others.
- Talk to Him with transparent honesty.
- Let intimacy with Him fuel your call to others.
- Be sure your thirst is for Jesus and not for human recognition.
- Build your foundation for intercession upon worship in spirit and truth rather than what you see in the natural.
- Be available to drop everything when He gives you an assignment.
- Be real with others.
- Decide that you will live to do His will and accomplish His work rather than your own.
- Keep on sowing until you reap a harvest, knowing that the fruit will be eternal.
- Cultivate an attitude of gratitude by recognizing that others have sown into the same soil from which you are reaping the harvest.
- Be prepared to go public with the things that God shows you in private.

- Believe God can use you to lead others and follow Him closely.
- Remember that if you are going to be a bridge for Jesus, at times you will feel overshadowed and overrun by those you are called to carry.
- Realize that if you've truly conveyed Christ, the focus won't be on what you have revealed but on the One who revealed it to you.
- Accept the fact that no one may ever know or remember your name on Earth, but your impact and reward can still be eternal.

A diamond is merely a piece of coal that has been through years and years of intense fire and pressure. If God has allowed you to go through much suffering and persecution, you can be sure that He will use the hurts and mistakes of your past and present to help a suffering people group. You need only thirst after His righteousness in prayer.

Isaiah 61:3 says that He came to bring beauty from the ashes. The places where you have been burned up, burned down, burned out—those are the places where you will discover the gift of intercession and service you are to share with others. Like the heavy stone of Jerusalem, God may have a people group that only you can pick up.

There now with the grace of God, go you!

————— **PERSONAL REFLECTION** —————

Are You a People-Group or Israel Intercessor?

1. Are you drawn to a particular group of people based on background, status, residence, occupation, health, knowledge, religion, race or nationality?

2. Has the Lord used difficult circumstances in your life to become a platform for your prayer life?

3. Have you been wounded by a people group? If so, though man meant it for evil, can you now ask God how He can use that wound for His glory and your good?

4. Has the Lord given you a love for Israel, God's first-born? Will you pick up the heavy stone?

5. Do you identify with the heart of mercy toward a people group? Which one?

6. Where have you been called to be a bridge and what price will you pay for that people group?

Note
1. Luis Bush and Beverly Pegus, *The Move of the Holy Spirit in the 10/40 Window* (Seattle: YWAM Publishing, 1999), pp. 118-120.

CHAPTER 12

PROPHETIC INTERCESSORS

GOD'S PRAYER ANCHORS

Television anchors today are literally wired to the commands of their producers. Most wear a custom-fitted earpiece called an IFB. This unique device is concealed from the viewing audience but is the lifeline between the person out front reporting news coverage and the producer behind the scenes directing it. Through the IFB, the anchor hears, speaks, sees and obeys what the producer directs. Prophetic intercession is much like being fitted for an IFB linked to God in order to report personal, local, national and global news and events.

My (Beth's) primary anointing in prayer is that of a prophetic intercessor. In other words, I pray the things on God's heart; then, under His direction, I report the words, thoughts, images and actions He releases me to share. Sometimes I will look at a person and see an image regarding his or her life that only the individual involved and God can explain. My job is to obey His instructions, refusing to speak outside the confines of what He has given me—but it wasn't always like that. I'll explain.

Baby Steps

Nothing is born full grown—not even the calling of God. All things mature through the process of either choices or time, or sometimes both! Prophetic intercession and prophetic giftings are no different. When God first spoke to the prophet Samuel as a boy, Samuel thought the voice he heard was coming from Eli the priest, his mentor (read 1 Samuel 3). The Lord made three attempts to speak before Samuel actually took his focus away from a human and directed it toward God. Surprisingly, the Lord pursued Samuel, even in his immaturity—what a comforting thought for those who are just learning to hear His voice and are relying instead on the counsel of others.

As we read on, we discover a major stumbling block for those who are learning to lean on God in prophetic intercession. The Bible says that "Samuel was afraid to tell the vision to Eli" (1 Sam. 3:15). In other words, the fear of human disapproval overshadowed the revelation of God. Everyone who is called to prophetic intercession must take the ax to the root of the "man-pleasing" spirit. For some, this will mean years and years of hacking away at it; for others, the process will be much simpler. Each person's background will require a different set of choices and seasons to uproot it.

It's interesting to note, however, that Eli was able to discern that Samuel was hiding something. When the painfully candid report was given, Eli confirmed its validity. The important point in this passage is that Eli told Samuel to lie down and listen to

God (see v. 9). Prophetic intercession is always birthed out of being still and hearing God's heart.

MY MENTOR, MY ELI

I (Beth) had a mentor who walked as Eli, attending to the intimate things upon God's heart. In my early Christian life, it seemed the Spirit of the Lord never impressed anything revelatory upon me. Then one day, Vinita Copeland, my mentor, called and asked me to pray for her about a specific need. I had been complaining to the Lord for not sharing with me in advance how He wanted me to pray. Nonetheless, I pursued His heart. Suddenly, the Lord showed me something in my spirit for Vinita. As I continued to pray, the floodgates of revelation gushed with fresh insight. When He finished speaking, I raced over to Vinita's house to share what I had perceived. Vinita listened intently and then excused herself so she could privately meet with the Lord.

I could hear her praying for a long time and thought, *My, the Lord is really dealing with her!* When she finally came out of her prayer room, I could see that she had been crying. I thought, *This is getting to her more than I realized it would.*

"Beth," she said, "come and sit down. Let's talk. This is what I shared with you. . . . This is what the Lord spoke to your heart. . . . This is what you added because you knew me. . . . And this what you added because you love me. . . ." I began to cry. She went on to say, "You have wondered why the Lord does not give you things in advance and this is why: He wants to keep His words pure. Therefore, until you have been purified, He is not going to let you know anything in advance. Remember, Beth, He wants your intercession to be a walk of faith and trust in Him."

As the seasons and choices of my life have passed, I have come to understand that prophetic intercession grows with trust.

The Secrets of God

Maturing in prophetic intercession means being trustworthy with the secrets of God, even if one's own reputation must be bruised in the process. It is refusing to breach His confidences—no matter what. We are to be like vaults where God can hide His private words and thoughts, knowing that they will only be released at His discretion. These words and thoughts are given to us so that His will can be prayed with accuracy upon the earth. We don't add to or brag about what He has placed in the vault, nor do we invite others in to see what God has preserved there.

We are to be like vaults where God can hide His private words and thoughts, knowing that they will only be released at His discretion.

The prophet Isaiah rebuked Hezekiah for showing the wealth of his treasury to the king of Babylon. Isaiah predicted that Judah's people and prosperity would be carried away because of that self-exalting act (see Isa. 39). Sadly, Hezekiah was more concerned about looking good than protecting the people and provision of God. Similarly, our prophetic mantle in prayer is secured through faith and trust in the things that mean the most to Him.

As we grow in the area of trust, we find that we are praying what Jesus would pray if He were physically here. The Lord may provide a passage of Scripture to pray that speaks directly from His heart to a situation. He may give us images and pictures during our times of prayer that represent His heart. Later, He may also ask us to share them publicly with others. He is the One, however, who decides the timing for opening the vault! We need only be prepared by staying close to Him.

Born Out of Prayer

Prophetic intercession is not something an intercessor conjures up; it is a choice to surrender to the heartbeat of God in prayer. It is the result of nestling your ear up against His heart to hear the things that cause Him hurt, happiness, frustration—all the emotions that we feel. As we lay aside our own agendas for His sake in prayer, we can expect to encounter the spirit of prophecy for the people, places and situations that He wants to speak to through our intercession.

All prophetic intercession points to Jesus. Isaiah 11:1,2 says that "the Spirit of the LORD will rest on Him, the spirit of wisdom and understanding, the spirit of counsel and strength, the spirit of knowledge and the fear of the LORD." While this Scripture points to Jesus' testimony, as His heirs we now lay hold of His testimony in prophetic intercession.

When the Holy Spirit is praying prophetically through one of His intercessors, the intent is always to protect, purify and prosper His Bride, the Church. First Corinthians 14:22 validates the Lord's intention: "prophecy is for a sign, not to unbelievers, but to those who believe." Why? Because prophecy releases faith, and faith moves mountains for God.

The Attitude of the Prophetic Intercessor

Everything God does, He does for one reason: He loves people! Therefore, when the Lord calls a prophetic intercessor into prayer, the attitude of that person must identify with God's heart in the matter. God does not call us into intercession to harm people; He calls us to cover them with His love, even when they are in the wrong (see 1 Pet. 4:8; Gal. 6:1). He pursues those who are lost in sin (see Luke 15:4); He extends forgiveness to those who confess their wrong (see Jas. 5:16); He comforts those who are mourning (see Matt. 5:4); He gives rest to those who are heavy laden (see Matt. 11:28); He satisfies those who are thirsty (see John 7:37); He strengthens those who are weak (see Isa. 40:28-31); He heals those who are sick (see Ps. 103:3); He gives wisdom to those who are seeking (see Jas. 1:5); He confronts those who are in denial (see 2 Sam. 12:7ff.); He judges those who unrepentantly harm His loved ones (see Ps. 34:16,21). Prophetic intercession will manifest the same kind of grace.

He is the One who said, "Eye has not seen and ear has not heard, . . . [nor has] entered the heart of man, all that God has prepared for those who love Him" (1 Cor. 2:9). The heart of the prophetic intercessor is to see the unseen and hear the unheard things that have not yet entered people's hearts so they will know, to an even greater depth, the love that God has for them.

Before we touch the things of God or seek His face, we must make sure that our hearts have been purified and our hands are clean. Psalm 24 says:

> And who may stand in His holy place? He who has clean hands and a pure heart, who has not lifted up his soul to falsehood, and has not sworn deceitfully. He shall receive a blessing from the LORD and righteousness from the God of his salvation. This is the generation of those who seek Him, who seek Thy face (vv. 3-6).

Prophetic intercession should always be preceded with a heart attitude of the Davidic prayer found in Psalm 139:

> Search me, O God, and know my heart; try me and know my anxious thoughts; and see if there be any hurtful way in me, and lead me in the everlasting way (vv. 23,24).

The everlasting way is the way that is focused on Christ and His holiness. Every attitude, every thought, every action of prophetic intercession should magnify God and not self.

Authority and Prophetic Intercession

Prophetic intercession is always submitted first to God's sovereign authority and then to His delegated authority. In other words, until the prophetic intercessor is under authority, that person is not equipped to assume the role of authority, even in intercession. This is because that authority is given for the purpose of protection, and to be outside of God's protection is to subject others to possible harm.

∞

𝒜uthority is given for the purpose of protection, and to be outside of God's protection is to subject others to possible harm.

∞

Authority is part of the prophetic call, which is to be a watchman for the Church so that it will not become enslaved (see 2 Pet. 2:18,19). Watchmen are those who keep the right people in and the wrong people out by lining up with God's authoritative chain of command. And a believer's call to the prophetic will be recognized by those in authority. For example, before the prophet Elijah ascended into heaven, he passed on his prophetic mantle to Elisha because Elisha had been a man under authority. Often prophetic intercessors who have been validated by authority will be solidified through the laying on of hands and/or the anointing with oil. This is what is called a prophetic or symbolic act, calling forth the authority in the natural that has already been recognized in the spiritual. It is an act of obedience to what God has spoken.

REVELATION, SPOKEN AND SEEN

God speaks to and through His prophetic intercessors in a multitude of ways: prayers, dreams, visions, songs, proclamations, symbolism and prophetic acts. Before anything occurs in the natural, it is first released in the spiritual realm.

God may use dreams to speak prophetically as He did with Jacob at Luz when he saw the ladder set on Earth that extended to heaven and heard the Lord's promises for His future blessing (see Gen. 28:12-16). The Lord may, however, give us a vision during our waking hours and allow us to see a picture of something that He is doing in the present or future. He may even give both. In Numbers 12:6, the Lord came down in a pillar of cloud and said to Miriam and Aaron, "Hear now My words: If there is a prophet among you, I, the LORD, shall make Myself known to him in a vision. I shall speak with him in a dream."

You may have had a dream or vision that you only partially understand. Write it down (see Hab. 2:2). The Lord may give you the vision in pieces, depending on what you can handle at the moment, or for some reason that He has a right to sovereignly withhold. Trust that if He gives it to you, He will also give you its interpretation at the appropriate time. Make this a matter of intercession.

Prophetic Proclamations

One way the Lord releases His will into situations is through prophetic proclamations, meaning that we speak God's perfect will into the unseen to call forth the seen things of the future. A prophetic proclamation is an official announcement of God's Word into the heavenlies—a declaration of faith based upon God's Word. When the Lord formed the earth, He did it through a proclamation (see Gen. 1). His spoken word bought forth His designated will for the earth. Today He makes proclamations through His people. Whenever a prophetic intercessor prays

God's written Word in faith over a person or situation, the faith of that person unites with the power of God's Word to release a creative combination upon the earth.

Prophetic proclamations begin with intercession. Thus, when a prophetic intercessory anointing is combined with people groups, for example, the Lord will provide a Scripture that is birthed out of His heart to proclaim over them. God may provide a proclamation to speak over a city, a state or a nation (see Ezek. 36:1,4). The prophet Isaiah says, "Get yourself up on a high mountain, O Zion, bearer of good news, lift up your voice mightily, O Jerusalem, bearer of good news; lift it up, do not fear. Say to the cities of Judah, 'Here is your God!'" (Isa. 40:9).

The Lord commanded Ezekiel to proclaim to the dry bones that they would come together as human flesh and carry the breath of God. This prophetic proclamation was commanded to restore hope to the spiritually parched and despairing house of Israel (see Ezek. 37).

Seeing the evidence of the proclamation is not nearly as important as knowing that God has instructed it and we have spoken it on His behalf. When Jesus proclaimed His will and cursed the fig tree in Mark 11, the tree did not change immediately, but His proclamation did manifest the evidence of His faith and His Word only one day later. Some proclamations are not evidenced for hundreds of years; that shouldn't matter. The obedience is far more important than the outcome. We are not responsible for the result of the proclamation but only for the obedience to speak it forth.

Learn to pray God's Word. We think of it like this: God is our Father and we are to say what our Father says. God has promised that His Word will not return void (see Isa. 55:11). And God is bound by His Word to honor His Word; He is not bound by our word. Therefore, only when we say what He says, as led by the Holy Spirit, is that word binding.

Jesus said that "if you have faith as a mustard seed, you shall say to this mountain, 'Move from here to there,' and it shall move; and nothing shall be impossible to you" (Matt. 17:20). Then in Jeremiah 23:29 we read, "'Is not My word like fire?' declares the LORD, 'and like a hammer which shatters a rock?'" Here again we find that our faith combined with His Word can burn away and break down the mountains of hindrance and blockage that confront His will from coming to pass upon the earth.

Prophetic Song

Prophetic proclamations can also come through song. One of the reasons prophetic intercession commonly joins with the anointing of worship intercession is to strengthen the Body. Though we have addressed the issue of worship intercession in chapter 10, we want to call attention to the fact that when worship combines with the prophetic, it can be both foretelling as well as forthtelling.

Many of today's great songwriters, such as Terry MacAlmon and Steve Fry, give credence to the fact that God shares the messages of His heart through prophetic intercession in song. Prophetic intercession through song can bring comfort, salvation, healing, joy, deliverance and victory.

Prophetic Acts

Another way that God will ask His prophetic intercessors to usher in His will is through prophetic acts, or tangible symbolic representations of things that He either does not want to be forgotten or things that He will bring to pass. The following are only a few of the prophetic acts of the Old and New Testaments:

- Moses was told to lift up the serpent on a stick for those who were sick. This prophetic act would ultimately represent Christ upon the cross, taking our sins upon Himself to render the healing of body, soul and spirit (see Num. 21:8,9).
- Moses commanded the Israelites to place the blood of a lamb upon the doorposts of the Jews so the angel of death would pass over. This prophetic act was symbolic of Christ, the Lamb of God, and the fact that His shed blood over our lives will result in eternal life (see Exod. 12:22,23).
- Ezekiel was told to take a brick, write Israel upon it and lay siege upon the brick. This prophetic act was to represent an attack against Israel (see Ezek. 4:1-3).
- Ezekiel was also commanded to take two sticks and write on one "For Judah and for the sons of Israel, his companions" and on the other "For Joseph, the stick of Ephraim and all the house of Israel, his companions." Ezekiel was told to join the two sticks as one. This prophetic act was to represent the Jews being brought together as one nation (see Ezek. 37:16-22).
- Ahijah the Shilonite prophet took his new cloak and tore it into 12 pieces. This prophetic act represented the dividing of Israel into 12 tribes (see 1 Kings 11:30-39).
- An unnamed woman broke an alabaster vial of costly perfume and poured it upon Jesus' head. This prophetic act symbolized Jesus' burial (see Mark 14:3,8).
- Jesus was baptized in the Jordan River. This prophetic act symbolized His death, burial and resurrection.

We perform this prophetic act to demonstrate that we acknowledge the power of His death, burial and resurrection in our own lives (see Matt. 3:13; Luke 3:21; Acts 2:38).

- The Lord's Supper, also known as Communion, was presented by Christ to symbolize our acceptance of His broken body and shed blood in payment for our sins. This prophetic act is a reminder that, as someone appropriately said, "He paid a debt He did not owe for people who owed a debt they could not pay" (see Mark 14:22-24; 1 Cor. 11:24-26).
- Agabus took Paul's belt and bound his own feet and hands. This prophetic act symbolized the way the Jews at Jerusalem would bind Paul and deliver him into the hands of the Gentiles (see Acts 21:10,11).

A Prophetic Prayer Journey

In 1996, Walter Heidenreich, a renowned German evangelist, called me (Beth) to share a prophetic dream he had received. In the dream the Lord said, "I will give you the youth of Mongolia if you will take your worship team into the heart of the Gobi Desert and worship me as King of kings and Lord of lords." Walter asked if Intercessors International would join his team to become the Lord's weapon for breaking strongholds over Mongolia. God assured me that Tommi, Jean Krisle and I were indeed to be a threefold cord of intercession there.

As I prayed, the Lord impressed upon me that I had a twofold purpose. I was not only to go as an intercessor, but also as a prophet to proclaim and call forth the oracles of God for the nation of Mongolia. I asked Walter if he would permit me to include some prophetic acts. He assured me that he would not object as long as the concert would not be hindered in any way. I agreed.

The Birthing of God's Plan

In the meantime, the Lord began to reveal an embryonic picture of His plan. I had prayed about the items I should take and God confirmed what I sensed through several of His spiritual leaders.

One Sunday, my pastor, Burton Stokes, sensed that God wanted us to give Communion to the ground as a prophetic act that would symbolize the cleansing of Mongolian land. As I pondered this in my heart, it began to resonate. A holy hush fell over me that glorious morning as the congregation sang "Lord Be Exalted Among the Nations." I wept in intercession and worship. As I did, the Holy Spirit prodded me to ask for a copy of the song on cassette tape. I had a sense that the concert would be in three parts: what was, what is and what is to come. Later, we saw the result of that revelation.

The day of departure finally arrived and I boarded a plane for Germany with a suitcase full of symbols for a yet-to-be-revealed purpose. The items included two majestic hand banners assembled by Quinett Simmons, Jane Hansen's book *Inside a Woman*, a handkerchief, Communion elements and a cassette recording of "Lord Be Exalted Among the Nations." The Holy Spirit was clearly in charge.

The Research

Prior to the trip, Steve Hawthorne, author of *Prayerwalking*, talked to Tommi after a speaking engagement in her home church. Steve explained that the Gobi Desert was originally a deep ocean, representing the fullness of God. Now, however, it is a desert, representing the absence of God's fullness. Presently the land of the Gobi is the desert furthest from any ocean. It may very well be one of the "waterless places" mentioned by Jesus in Matthew 12:43-45.

Steve pointed out that demonic activity in such areas could be strong in different ways from what we often encounter in inhabited cities. By this way of viewing the Gobi, it may be a staging ground of disembodied powers of darkness who are exiled, angered or eager to again dominate humans and their places of habitation. He urged us to consider that our assignment may be to "only" worship and celebrate the Lord, and not to do confrontive warfare.

Our research intercessors had also been summoned to provide us with strategic knowledge about the prevailing spirits over the land as well as other useful historical and geographical facts about the Gobi Desert. Their investigation revealed that Ghengis Khan had conquered and united the nation of Mongolia through violence and had extended the Mongolian Empire from Poland to Korea and from the middle of Russia to China. One of the reigning spirits is violence (Mongolia had at that time the highest rate of violence in the world). The Scripture for our proclamation was to be Isaiah 60:16-18, which ends with, "Violence will not be heard again in your land, nor devastation or destruction within your borders; but you will call your walls salvation, and your gates praise (v. 18)."

The research intercessors also found that Kublai Khan, Ghengis's grandson, had been pursuing truth and asked Marco Polo to send Christians to his nation. His request was denied! Mongolia had given a Macedonian call that had remained unanswered for generations.

Mongolia, Beauty Shrouded in Darkness

The 19-hour flight from Germany to the capital of Mongolia, Ulaanbaatar, was exhausting. Once in Ulaanbaatar, we met with the HELP International team, an outreach from Walter Heidenreich's ministry stationed in Mongolia to minister to alcoholics, drug addicts and abandoned children.

We traveled on to Dalanzadgad where we joined the 15-member band that was to accompany us for God's private concert. Driving to our quarters, we saw mounds of prayer rocks piled high and topped with flags to honor the various gods of the land.

On the day of the concert, we spent much time preparing the things we would need for this historical occasion. The Lord impressed Walter to build an altar of stones as a memorial, just as the Israelites had done under the old covenant to commemorate a truth or an event. Twenty-four large stones were gathered. A sense of destiny engulfed me as I prayed and called out the names of the 12 tribes of Israel and the 12 apostles for Walter while he wrote them one by one on each of the rocks.

Wood is a scarce and precious commodity in the Gobi, so we purchased two fence boards from a Mongolian family. We had just enough to build a five-foot-high and four-foot-wide wooden cross. After the words "Jesus ist Herr" (Jesus is Lord) were written on one side of the cross, the Lord began to unveil the purpose for the symbolic treasures I had brought from home.

I handed one of Quinett's beautifully sequined and braided banners to Walter. It was shaped like a crown and carried a majestic truth: KING JESUS! Walter nailed the banner over the cross while those of us in attendance rejoiced. We all believed the banner was an important visual proclamation of Jesus' lordship in crowning Him King over the land. I knew that the altar we would build signified a powerful event for Mongolia greater than any of us could imagine. It was prophetic; I knew it was God!

Destination Gobi

At long last, our caravan of five jeeps and a truck loaded with 18 people, numerous musical instruments, sound equipment, supplies and even a generator launched on a mission that only God could have orchestrated.

When we arrived, Walter and the musicians needed a couple of hours to set up, so Tommi, Jean and I took that time to bury Jane Hansen's book on behalf of Aglow International. As we dug into the warm sandy soil, we prayed that God's Spirit would be placed inside the hearts of the Mongolian women to ignite a desire for intimacy with Him. We called forth the women of Mongolia to proclaim the gospel and lay hold of their freedom.

The Cross—What Was

Walter finally called us to gather around the vacant hole that had been hollowed out of the Gobi sand to couch the sacred cross. The rocks prepared for the altar lay nearby to be used as a memorial around its stem.

Walter asked me to lead the Communion service. Jean offered a prophetic prayer and placed the bread in the ground; I poured the wine, symbolizing the spiritual cleansing of the land. I then placed the cassette tape on top of the handkerchief and proclaimed a change in the hold that rock music has upon the

Earth, announcing into the heavenlies that Mongolia would sing forth the oracles of God and that a change would occur as the ground sings forth the praises of the Lord.

Walter's wife, Irene, reverently laid her beloved Bible in the ground, proclaiming that God's Word would go forth across the land of Mongolia. It was indeed a solemn moment, one that we knew was chronicled in heaven. The precious prophetic items now rested in the pregnant sand. The 24 stones were carefully stacked around the cross. It dawned on me that I had one more prophetic act to complete. Walter nodded in agreement.

I poured oil on the thirsty ground as I marched around the cross, declaring that the Lord would encircle that place with His power and that He would guard the prophetic acts completed there. I asked the Lord to encircle the Mongolian people just as I had encircled the cross.

No one was ready for what happened next! As Helmut steadied the cross, Jost began to hammer the timber into the stubborn Mongolian soil, using a large heavy mallet. Each fierce blow pierced the depths of our souls as we were spiritually enveloped by the sounds of Golgotha's gruesome spikes being driven into Jesus' outstretched arms and blood-drenched feet, the holiness of the ages hinging upon one prophetic moment—Calvary!

My heart writhed in pain as I realized *He did this for me!* Holy, holy, holy. I stood there stunned with awe, then fell upon my face.

Tommi later confessed, "When the sound of the mallet hit the cross, it echoed like rumbling thunder over the land. The stillness of the desert awakened with life. My mind whisked me off to Calvary. I felt as though I was there. I felt so unworthy, so unclean, so full of sin and shame. I wondered, *Why me? Why am I here? I don't belong.* Confusion set in. *What should I be doing? I know I'm here as an intercessor, but should I worship? Can I worship?* I wanted to flee. I wanted to be as far removed from this convicting scene as possible."

The Concert—What Is

As the concert began, the presence of God fell mightily upon the land. My body dropped with a holy thud under a deep sense of conviction as I once again remembered the Cross. Suddenly I understood what the prophet Isaiah meant when he said, "all our righteous deeds are like a filthy garment" (Isa. 64:6). I cried out for mercy and He sent His love. It was as tangible as life itself. I have never felt so insignificant and yet so completely loved.

Swept away in His joy, I began to dance, whirling before Him. For a split second I saw the heavens open and what seemed to be a large coliseum etched out of polished white marble. I saw a cloud of heavenly witnesses in holy array. As I looked closer, I recognized loved ones who had crossed into eternity. I could see my mother, my grandmothers and my spiritual mother, Vinita Copeland. She appeared regal! In an instant it was over. Again I was back on my face before my awesome God, worshiping Him on holy ground.

Jean Krisle later said, "I, too, was caught up in an open heaven. The Lord showed me that His divine protection had faithfully engulfed us. 'This is Mine,' He said, 'and I am watching over it.' Twenty-four years of my unwavering intercession against rock music culminated in one holy event; I was honored to be a part of it. I could feel the absolute presence of God and the absence of man. The Holy Spirit choreographed every sequence of this divinely appointed concert. It was awesome!"

We could all feel the presence of heavenly hosts in our midst.

The Proclamation—What Is to Come

I glanced at Tommi, whose face now shone radiantly with the glory of the Lord. Tommi moved toward Walter to whisper that the Lord had given her a proclamation from Song of Solomon 2:8-12. He fell on his face like a rag soaked in tears of heavenly worship. When he finally rose, he called Tommi to the microphone to pray over Mongolia. Tommi set the proclamation aside in submission to God's servant, praying a prayer that carried the authority of Christ for the Mongolian people and nation. The prayer then launched into a proclamation. Tears were coursing down Tommi's cheeks as she announced, "Mongolia, you are part of the Bride who will hear the turtle dove calling . . . you will no longer be naked and ashamed . . . rejoice, Mongolia, and respond to the Bridegroom, and know Him as the One who loves you."

The spirit of intercession welled up among the group. Jean proclaimed that Mongolia would sing a new song as she sang forth the words of Psalm 96. I proclaimed that God would raise up mighty spiritual leaders in the nation to lead the government, the churches, the men, the women and the children that had been planted upon all regions of Mongolian soil.

We faced the north, south, east and west, calling for spiritual sons and daughters to come in. We called for the Bride. The band joined in with a prophetic song of proclamation as we all cried out in one prophetic voice, "You're free, Mongolia, you're free!"

A sense of victory burst forth with such exhilaration that Walter took off running and leaping across the endless sea of sand dunes. Jean and I swooped up a banner and raced across the dusty sand, waving the banner's imposing message over the parched earth beneath our feet: RIVERS OF LIVING WATER! Tommi stood in the background proclaiming, "The seed will grow well, the vine will yield its fruit, the ground will produce its crops, and the heavens will drop their dew."

God's Finale

Like a blanket of glory peeling back the reality below, the concert met its closing moment. Then the final blessing! When the jeeps were fully loaded and we sojourners were still basking in His wonder, heavy rain clouds gathered in the sky.

As we barreled over the Gobi landscape, God ignited the skies with an unparalleled performance in the heavens. Spears of lightning punctured the ripe clouds as the thirsty ground swallowed up the promised latter rain. That night the desert flooded. God's will had been accomplished in Mongolia and He was well pleased!

Jean, Tommi and I flopped into bed that evening drained from the staggering emotion of time spent in His presence. Each of us were lying there in a spirit of intercession when, almost on cue, we burst forth in warfare. It soon subsided and one by one we fell asleep.

About 2 A.M., I awoke with a start from a prophetic dream. Three angels descended upon the holy place where we had worshiped. They scooped up the cross, along with the symbolic articles from our prophetic acts, including the 24 rocks with the names of the 24 elders written upon them. I saw the angels flying with majestic grace through the heavenlies until they reached the feet of the One who sat upon the throne. There, all was laid at the feet of Jesus.

One week after our trip, I visited a castle in Germany. Hanging on the decorated wall before me was a painting of three angels carrying a church to heaven. They carried it exactly as the ones who carried away the cross in my God-given dream. Again, I could hear the Father saying, "Behold, I am well pleased!

The following year, Walter hosted the first conference of any kind ever to be held in Mongolia. Two thousand youth attended and, with crushing power, all charged to the altar to give their lives to Jesus. Walter now has an open-door policy with the nation's president to minister in Mongolian schools and prisons. Within two years of the concert, the ministry has recorded 32,000 converts; Walter has also planted a Mongolian prison church. God answered Kublai Khan's Macedonian call through one man's obedience to a prophetic dream!

Pitfalls of Prophetic Intercessors

Prophetic intercessors are those who are called to prepare the way for God's will to be done upon the earth. A problem can arise, however, when these intercessors fall into the trap of thinking that they have to explain everything before they pray it or perform it. This is but one of the many pitfalls that encumber prophetic intercession. Others include:

- Finding identity in the prophetic rather than in God who gives it
- Adding to or subtracting from what God has said in order to either look knowledgeable or to keep from looking ridiculous
- Refusing to allow the prophetic word or act to undergo the scrutiny of authority

- Getting into "one-upmanship" by trying to outdo the previous prophetic prayer, word or deed
- Adding personal opinions or impressions that can bring judgment over a person, a people group or a land
- Sharing secrets that God has not okayed
- Speculating about God's time frame or other details
- Owning the prophetic word or act rather than releasing it to God's long-range purpose
- Attributing more authority to self than to God, and thereby becoming puffed up
- Spending too little time in the prayer closet when God opens the door to go public
- Forgetting that many of the biblical prophets were ridiculed and stoned for their obedience
- Refusing to give a word because of jealousy
- Falling prey to intimidation or unbelief

Moses, the Profile of a Prophetic Intercessor

No other prophet of God is held in higher esteem among Christians and Jews alike than Moses, the only one who is credited with having seen the Lord face-to-face (see Exod. 33:11). Every prophetic intercessor will find deep, rich nuggets of wisdom embedded in the study of Moses' life. God Himself said that His conversations with Moses were "just as a man speaks to his friend" (v. 11).

The relationship began on God's behalf long before Moses' mother tucked him away in a reed-woven "ark" upon the crocodile-infested waters of the Nile. God had flushed his life through the whimpering birth canal of a people who longed for a deliverer. An Egyptian pharaoh's hand would rock his cradle, while the mother who loved him enough to give him up would nurse him in the palace. Moses' life began in peril and scrolled through the decades with sorrow upon sorrow, but that pain-strewn history became what the Jews call *michayil al chayil* (strength to strength).

Moses was an Israelite adopted by the pharaoh of Egypt and groomed to be a prince. But Prince Moses relinquished his royal heritage when God promised that he would be used to bring deliverance to his Israelite brethren. Moses was 40 years old when God gave him that prophetic promise. Surely he was the man for the job—one look at his résumé proved that! So Moses gave all his human strength and natural ability to the task. He proceeded to fulfill the word of the Lord by single-handedly killing a back-slashing Egyptian slave master—and in one self-directed act became a notorious fugitive in Egypt, wanted for murder. The prince in the palace was now the bounty hunter's prey.

Our microwave mentalities often cause us to forget that *process* is typically part of God's provision as He raises us up in prophetic intercession—and the process takes time! But messes usually lead to our message and our detours are not dead ends; they merely become part of the training ground in our passage to God's purposes. Like Moses, we too can expect some delays in the desert of intercession where the sweat and tears that are forged there provide us with deeper intimacy and greater faith. It is in the desert that wrong motives are burned out of us and patience, trust and steadfastness are sealed in. God met Moses alone in the desert during a time when he least expected to see the Lord's glory—and so will we!

As we stretch the telescope of time back toward the life of Moses, we see that he turns aside to study a bush that is on fire but is not being consumed by the flames. God is about to teach him something that will change his life forever, and we too should take note. Bushes are consumed as their own energy is used up. This bush was indwelt with the energy of God. God burned *through* the bush while the energy of the bush remained at rest. This illustration is branded into the pages of biblical history so that we might remember: It is His power in us, not our power, that brings about prophetic intercession and the acts that accompany it! Let's look at some of the other lessons to be gleaned from Moses' life:

- Be willing to give up everything and go wherever He directs!
- Don't argue with God.
- A bad past does not disqualify you for a prophetic future, so refuse to stare at the rearview mirror.
- If your life has been imperiled with deep wounds, trust that God will use the depth of your dependence upon Him to prophetically lead others in a pathway of deliverance.
- Don't be so holy and separate that you're afraid to get dirty from the sheep—love them, touch them, serve them.
- Recognize that interceding for dirty sheep is a way to find friendship with a holy God.
- Make sure that your intercession is filled with love for the rebellious.
- Stand in the gap for the iniquities of others.
- Be sure to tell God that if He doesn't go with you, you won't go either.
- Know that God is Lord over those who oppose you.
- Expect God to show up in the ordinary with His extraordinary power.
- Be on the alert to His voice even in desert times.

- Be real in God's presence and take off the robes of self-effort.
- Take off the shoes of your human authority in His presence so He can endow you with renewed authority for His future plans.
- Pick up your authority when God says it's time, knowing that others will recognize it.
- Focus on who He is and not on human intellect or education.
- Refuse to substitute action for intimate intercession.
- Allow commitment to the Lord to drive away all intimidation or fear.
- Realize that when you've had the greatest times in prayer, others are most apt to shock you with the works of idolatrous hands.
- Even if you blow it, run to God for renewed strength, and restore broken relationships with people.
- Ask God to give you a hunger and a thirst for holiness.
- Know that even those who are closest to you may become jealous, but God is big enough to set the record straight.
- Stay submitted to authority, no matter how sure you are that you have heard God's plan.
- Seek and follow wise counsel.
- Don't take credit for what God gives through you.
- Cultivate a love for prophetic song.
- Say yes to mentoring others who are pursuing prophetic prayer so He can multiply His life through you for future generations.
- Beware of adding to or subtracting from the acts of a holy God, realizing that disobedience can block the gate to your promised land.

"I advise you to buy from Me gold refined by fire, that you may become rich, and white garments, that you may clothe yourself, and that the shame of your nakedness may not be revealed; and eye salve to anoint your eyes, that you may see" (Rev. 3:18). This is the advice of the One who sits upon the throne of heaven to send forth prophetic acts and intercession.

Moses bought the gold, the white garments and the eye salve. Will you?

PERSONAL REFLECTION

Are You a Prophetic Intercessor?

1. Are you praying the things on God's heart and, under His direction, reporting the words, thoughts, images and actions He releases you to share?
2. Can the Lord trust you to be a vault where He can hide His private words and thoughts, knowing they will only be released at His discretion?
3. Do people usually say that you prayed exactly what was on their hearts?
4. Are your prayers often reflective of what Scripture says over a person, place or thing?
5. Has your role of authority been recognized by those in authority?
6. Does God speak to you through dreams, visions, songs, proclamations, symbolism or prophetic acts?

CHAPTER 13

FINDING FOCUS AND FRIENDSHIP

∽

SMART-BOMB PRAYING

People who suffer creatively together make close bonds. Those who don't know how to bond to God and other people suffer in bondage. As Christians, we are hell's defectors who have escaped from the suffering of sin's isolating prison camps. We now have heaven's amnesty from Satan's deadly grip and the privilege of joining God's army as those who are to loose others still tied by cords of wickedness and yokes of slavery (see Ps. 129:3,4; Isa. 58:6). We are part of an ongoing battle that must be fought in the spiritual realm to effect change in the physical (see Eph. 6:12).

The Bible says that Jesus is the vine and we are His branches (see John 15:5). Like the branch or rod Moses used to lead Israel out of bondage, bring water out of a rock and call forth God's power in battle, we are living branches raised up on various battlefields to carry His power. Therefore, we must know our place in intercession, take our authoritative position in that place and understand our purpose for being there.

The Rod of Intercessory Power

Moses knew where, when and how to do battle on God's behalf because he spent so much time in prayer and picked the right prayer partners. In Exodus 17, as the personalities of those he led are unveiled, we see one murmuring malcontent after another emerging. These thirsty Israelites want water and they want it yesterday! Moses is about to be stoned by his own people when God instructs him to surround himself with some friends and pick up his rod to strike the rock at Horeb. Water springs forth and flaring tempers are temporarily quenched.

Now, with the impassioned quarrel on the home front diffused, Moses catches another ominous whiff of trouble smoldering in Rephidim. The Amalekites, descendants of Esau, appear on the scene. These brawny brutes are in hot pursuit of Israel's blessing and birthright. But Moses goes straight to God for a strategy. Moses enlists his friend Joshua to handpick his own army that will accompany him in physical combat against the Amalekites. In the meantime, Moses, Aaron and Hur station themselves at the top of the hill to fight the battle in prayer.

With God's rod of triumph lifted up in his hands, Moses witnesses the power of the Lord descending upon Joshua. As long as Moses holds the rod up over the battlefield, Joshua's troops prevail. But Moses' arms grow heavy and his strength begins to wane. Each time Moses lowers the rod, the Amalekites gain some ground. Moses understands that he has been called to carry the prayer burden in this place and that he has been given the authority to uphold the rod of intercession. He dares not pawn off his position on another for the sake of comfort.

Aaron and Hur have also been commissioned by God to positions of authority in prayer. The Lord of Hosts has chosen both of these men to stand on either side of Moses to lift up his arms when he weakens. Though neither is called to be the general of this intercessory trio, the success Moses evokes on top of the hill depends on the ability of his companions to maintain their place beside him, giving support.

Moses, Aaron and Hur cannot win the battle without the efforts of Joshua and his men in the valley below—nor can Joshua gain the victory without the intercessory power from the hilltop above. Each person has a place to occupy on the battlefield; each one has a position to fill in that place; each place and position brings with it a level of authority against the enemy there. If one person moves outside of his place or position—if just one oversteps his authority—all will suffer the consequences.

Every Person Is Important

The battle at Rephidim bears witness to the fact that every single one of us is needed to partner in prayer with God and each other in order to defeat the efforts of Satan. Some of us will be called to the top of the hill to lead; others will be called there as part of a support team. Some will be sent to the front lines to fight, to bring mercy and healing to the wounded, to proclaim truth to the fainthearted, to spy out the land, to confront governing powers, to infiltrate enemy lines and to rescue those who are seeking a way of escape. All must take their rightful place in intercession and fearlessly uphold the borders of their position in order to win the war.

Why have so many fought for so long and so hard with such poor results? Like those who sought to stone Moses, many of us are too busy fighting amongst ourselves and complaining about our leaders to enter the battle. We have come to the front lines and hilltops of intercession so wounded and hurt that we have become rods of persecution rather than rods of God's power. Too many of us have tried to fight the battle alone and have lost! Even when all of these obstacles have been dealt with, one perilous oversight still exists: Few of God's people have understood where they are to fight, and thus they are bored with the battle.

The "Bored" Room of Prayer

In no other sector of the Church do we find people feeling more out of place and bored than in the prayer ministry. If God works through the prayers of His people, where are they? Prayer meetings often begin with a large, enthusiastic cadre of people, but dwindle to a scant few after only one or two meetings. You've probably attended at least one.

The most aggressive intercessor will often take over and pray through a list of problems for every person in his or her family. Several yawns later, another brave soul might chime in with a pressing governmental issue, while someone else begins to prophesy over the pastor or do battle against the principalities in the city. Confusion is rampant. Most people leave the meeting feeling unheard, unwanted or bored to tears!

This mind-numbing scenario is a far cry from the picture we see at Rephidim. Joshua and Moses both fought the same enemy but used different strengths on different battlefields to win the war. Why did they win? They were united in focus. They were not scattered all over the place. Joshua and his men carried the burden of warfare while Moses, Aaron and Hur carried the burden of a prophetic act coupled with intercession.

Your Burden, Your Battlefield

A young man once asked Mother Teresa how he could impact the world as powerfully as she had. Her reply was, "Find your Calcutta."[1] In other words, identify the people, places, issues or burdens that grieve your heart and create a passion in you or compel you to pray. Your burden is your battlefield.

Often what Satan has attempted to use to destroy us or our loved ones will become the battlefield where we are called to fight. Those who have victoriously emerged from the enemy's camp can usually identify the escape routes. That is not to say that we must always experience something to have a burden for it, but there is usually a common thread that weaves through the tapestry of our victory banners to identify our passions.

If you don't have a particular burden, ask the Lord for one. Here are some questions to help you identify your prayer burden—where you have been called to lift up your rod in intercession:

- Whose hurts do you identify with the most?
- Where do you see the most injustice happening?
- What issues do you identify with most?
- Which of God's leaders are most often on your mind?
- What nation do you think needs the most change?

• Where in this world would you most like to see God stretch forth His power rod for change?

Aligned to Become a Stronger Force

Once you have found your battlefield, affiliate with others who share your vision. Moses handpicked Joshua, Aaron and Hur. Joshua carefully chose the men who would join him on the front lines. These men were united. They did not look at the obstacles; they kept their eyes on the goal and supported each other.

When we have defined our battlefield, we must align ourselves with people who have the same vision. Lack of focus will always keep us from hitting our prayer target. That is why it is so important to connect with like-minded intercessors. God has only one army. That army, however, occupies thousands of outposts staffed with numerous positions of rank.

When hen we have defined our battlefield, we must align ourselves with people who have the same vision.

Some of us will spend our whole lives at one duty station; others will be moved from assignment to assignment. The key is to stay lined up under God, our Commander in Chief, and to move based on faith that we are on target with His plan for our lives. Romans 14:23 says that "whatever is not from faith is sin"—it is missing the mark. And faithfully hitting the mark will always require a prayer strategy.

Smart-Bomb Prayers

Before Moses sought the aid of Joshua, Aaron and Hur, he went to God for a plan. We, too, must be clear about the strategy for accomplishing our prayer assignments from God.

During the Vietnam War, my husband, Ralph, flew missions as a fighter pilot and witnessed enormous unnecessary destruction. I (Tommi) remember the men in his squadron using the term "dumb bombs," because they never knew if the bomb they dropped would hit the target. Too many variables had to be factored into the equation, such as the accuracy and skill of the pilot, the weather conditions and the target's naked-eye visibility.

America's random mass of military might underwent a major overhaul after Vietnam. Then in 1991, the Desert Storm war erupted. This time technology had given birth to weapons of warfare that depended on a different source than that of the pilot's accuracy—laser power. By condensing light into a focused stream of energy, dumb bombs were transformed into smart bombs! That light source could now be channeled so precisely that a pilot could place a bomb in an 18-x-18-inch air vent.

Other technological advances have also given strength to our military supremacy. We now have "FLIR," or "Forward Looking Infra Red." FLIR is used to detect even the slightest edge between light and darkness. It can pinpoint every kind of heat. The military uses it to expose not only people, but also anything else that might be camouflaged in darkness. With this infrared light, any dark image can be spotted and locked on as a designated target upon a radar screen. Once the pilot has a lock on the target, there is little hope of escape for the enemy.

For too many years, we Christians have been in the locked position. Satan has targeted us and condensed his streams of darkness to destroy our might within our families, cities and nations. These places have become his hot beds of destruction, and we have acted as though we had no hope of escape.

Thinking that we can't do everything, some of us have done nothing. Those who have been praying are usually spread too thin to be effectual. The truth is that if we as individuals become scattered in our prayer efforts, we won't be able to accomplish anything. But if each one of us connects in prayer with at least one or two others to form a threefold union like that of Moses, Aaron and Hur at Rephidim, we can streamline the light that God gives us to become a "smart bomb" against the enemy. The key is that we must connect with intercessors who share our focus and anointing, and then ask God to give us a strategy to put the lock on Satan.

Maintaining the Focus

Years ago, Tommi and I (Beth) were asked to train some Christians in strategic warfare. These people intended to retrace and reclaim for God the steps of Mao Zedong's notorious Long March that spread Communism throughout China. When we stepped off the train in Shenzen, we were aghast to learn of the strategies used by many poverty-stricken Chinese parents in that border town. There, the most outgoing and promising child in the family is intentionally maimed to become a beggar who will provide for the rest of the family.

We were especially drawn to the yearning cries of a little boy whose parents used a machete to cut off a portion of his arm. They continued to whack his head every few days so the fresh blood that seeped through his bandages would evoke pity in passersby. Many maimed children crowded around us as we sought to cancel Satan's lock on their lives with the light of Jesus' love in prayer.

As we forged our way through the oppressive streets of Shenzen, we met the flower girls. Young, fragile and malnourished, these 10- to 13-year-olds had already experienced the ravages of prostitution and known the excruciating pain of lost innocence. We stopped to tell the story of Jesus, and they listened with attentive ears. Each step we took led us into a greater web of sorrow. Our hearts almost became hostages to the misery that surrounded us. We had to tear ourselves away.

A scroungy-looking old man living under a bridge clamored for our attention. Deep furrows of despair etched this grandfather's face. His words rang with unforgettable passion as he pleaded with us to smuggle his tiny six-month-old grandbaby out of the country.

We longed to scoop all the children up into our arms—to rock them, to shelter them and to take them safely home to America. But that was not God's strategy. He had called us to teach others how to streamline their prayers so that the land could be healed. We had to stay focused on our mission. God had summoned other groups to bring food, medical supplies and Bibles, but that was not our course.

It can be a struggle at times to stay focused on the purpose God has given us. So many hurts, so few workers. The distraction of need beckons us at every corner. Without the support of our Joshuas, Aarons and Hurs, we can easily lose our focus. What if Moses had left the hilltop and rushed down to care for a wounded soldier at Rephidim? What if Aaron and Hur had argued over the celebrity of their positions? What if Joshua had looked at the hilltop above rather than the battlefield before him? These men won because they maintained their focus. What about you? What is God calling you to? Where is your focus?

Surviving the Enemy's Flak

Even those with a crystalline vision can expect to encounter flak. Desert Storm exposed this unsophisticated weaponry. Flak consists of many 2–4-inch shells that are shot into the air to explode at a preset altitude. Flak is discharged with the hope that an opposing airplane will fly into the chunks of metal that are randomly dispersed and that the metal will punch holes in the plane's fuel tanks or infiltrate and destroy the jet engines.

Flak is random stuff—a bunch of small or large stuff—that the enemy hopes we will run into just as we begin to gain momentum in reaching our purpose. Notice that flak is something we run into. We don't have to accept the enemy's flak. We don't have to let the small things he sends our way steal our energy or destroy our goals.

Someone once said that an obstacle is something we see when we take our eyes off the target. Prayer is the way we avoid flak and hit the target. Prayer helps us to line up with God's timing so that the preset discharge of our enemy's flak will miss us. We can do the right thing at the wrong time and still miss the target. But if we follow God's timing, we can know that Satan's flak will always be too early or too late to hit us.

During Desert Storm, America used SAMs—Surface to Air Missiles—to reckon with the enemy. The sophistication of SAMs was one of the many superior weapons that enabled the United States forces to end the war in record time.

When you and I set our feet on the soil, or surface, God has called us to, focusing our prayers on the targets He has assigned to us, our prayers become missiles—weapons of destruction to thwart the enemy's plans (see Ezek. 4:2). Prayer is the SAM of our spiritual warfare. Through prayer, the desert storms of the past

*S*omeone once said that an obstacle is something we see when we take our eyes off the target.

will become the launching pads for our future missions. We need only:

- Ask God for the prayer strategy.
- Accept our place on the battlefield.
- Affiliate with intercessors who share the same burden.
- Acknowledge and honor the prayer anointings of others.
- Anchor our prayer focus on the target God has given us.
- Align ourselves with God's timing through prayer.

The Bridal Invitation

When you have determined your own place of power in prayer, you will suddenly find that the anointings of others are also needed to complete the purposes and will of God. Only by helping others to find their place in the Body of Christ can we be certain of finding our own. His Body is much like a puzzle—until each one of us picks up our piece and finds our place, we cannot present a whole picture of Christ's Bride to the world.

Shortly after we started working on this book, God gave a prophetic dream of a radiant bride clothed in a long elegant gown. The train of the bridal dress shimmered with sparkling white diamonds, delicately beaded designs and intricately woven lace. Her veil was full and majestic. Worldly crowds carrying enticing gifts clamored for her attention, but the bride raced toward a staircase that called to her with compelling silent strength.

The last stair led to the palm of Christ's right hand; it was mammoth in size, exuding brilliant rays of holy light. As the bride fell into the Hand of God, she too was shrouded in the light. His body stood multiple stories high in stature, draped in a robe of glory. Gently raising the bride in His strong, protective hand, He placed it over His heart and held it there until she was enveloped in it. All self was gone as the bride was hidden in Christ. From that moment on, she merely rested in Him. She found the truth that "in quietness and trust is your strength" (Isa. 30:15)—no more striving.

We are the Body and Bride of Christ. So when we single-mindedly pursue His heart in prayer, we have all the anointing we need to make His will known to a lost and dying world. As one pastor prayed, "Blot us out, Lord, blot us out that the world may see JESUS ONLY!"

PERSONAL REFLECTION
Have You Found Your Focus?

1. Have you found your prayer-power mix as an intercessor on God's battlefield? Whose anointing do you need to connect with in order to fulfill your prayer purpose?

2. What are some of the old wounds that need healing in order to become a rod of God's prayer power rather than a rod of persecution?

3. What prayer battlefields has God called you to in the past? Did you pray "dumb bomb" or "smart bomb" prayers?

4. Do the people you are affiliated with share your prayer burden? If not, who does? How can you connect with those people?

5. Where are you resisting the call to be blotted out so that the world may see Jesus only?

Note
1. Jim Burns and Greg McKinnon, *Illustrations, Stories and Quotes* (Ventura, CA: Gospel Light Publications, 1997), p. 159.